Kindergarten: Ready or Not?

Contra Costa Child Care Council
1035 Detroit Ave., Ste. 200
Concord, CA 94518

Contra Costa Child Care Council
1035 Detroit Ave., Ste. 200
Concord, CA 94518

Kindergarten Ready or Not?

A PARENT'S GUIDE

Sean A. Walmsley

Bonnie Brown Walmsley

HEINEMANN
Portsmouth, NH

Heinemann
A division of Reed Elsevier Inc.
361 Hanover Street
Portsmouth, NH 03801-3912
Offices and agents throughout the world

Acquisitions Editor: Carolyn Coman
Production Editor: Renée M. Nicholls
Manufacturing: Louise Richardson
Cover and interior design: Jenny Jensen Greenleaf
Cover illustration: Colleen Trainor
Interior illustrations: Sean Smith, Zachary Kineke, Joshua Chew, Colleen Trainor, Tracy Naberezny, and Sean O'Brien

Library of Congress Cataloging-in-Publication Data

Walmsley, Sean A.
 Kindergarten: ready or not? A parent's guide / Sean A. Walmsley, Bonnie Brown Walmsley.
  p. cm.
 Includes bibliographical references (p.).
 ISBN 0-435-08860-2
 1. Kindergarten—United States. 2. Readiness for school—United States. I. Walmsley, Bonnie Brown. II. Title.
 LB1205.W35 1996
 372.21′8—dc20   96-19257
                                                         CIP

Printed in the United States of America on acid-free paper

03 02 01 00   DA   3 4 5 6 7 8

*This book is dedicated to Renita Toulon Brown,
Bonnie's mother, who trusted and encouraged
her children to discover the world for themselves
before kindergarten, and long afterward.*

Contents

Contents

Acknowledgments

We are grateful to a number of people and institutions for their assistance in writing this book, and this is the place where we can publicly thank them.

We appreciate the time and effort of teachers, parents, and early childhood educators who responded to our surveys. Even if their specific stories aren't found in this book, their concerns, expectations, and aspirations for children's kindergarten experiences are reflected here, and they've heightened our awareness of the issues we need to address.

We appreciate the time and effort of our colleagues Bernadine Starrs and her faculty at the Montessori School in Albany, NY, and Evelyn Barber and the other faculty members at the Spring Hill Waldorf School in Saratoga Springs, NY. We hope we've described their approaches fairly and accurately.

We appreciate the contributions of the following university and professional colleagues who helped us better understand kindergarten practices in other parts of the country as well as some of the research findings related to kindergarten: Dick Allington, Deborah May, and Anne McGill-Franzen at the University of New York at Albany; Mary Shake at the University of Kentucky; Abbey Weber, Rosendale School, Niskayuna, NY; Phyllis Aldrich, Coordinator, Gifted and Talented Program, Washington-Saratoga BOCES, Saratoga Springs, NY; and Mary Ellen Seitelman, President of Shenendehowa Advocates for Gifted Education, Clifton Park, NY.

We are also enormously grateful to the parents who shared their experiences with us. We can't thank them by name (and the names we use in this book aren't their real ones), but we do thank them. Their reward will be that someone else's child will benefit from their accounts.

Finally, we thank everyone at Heinemann who has made this book a reality, especially Carolyn Coman, Acquisitions Editor, who saw promise in the idea and guided it through the various stages of production. We also are grateful for the contributions of Nancy Bolick, Developmental Editor; Alan Huisman, Copy Editor; and Jenny Jensen Greenleaf, Designer.

Introduction

Not too long ago, our local paper ran an opinion piece chastising parents for holding their children out of kindergarten. Send them on time, the author advised, and everything will work out fine. Recently, a different writer weighed in, telling parents it was okay to hold their sons or daughters out. No need to hurry them into formal education; let them enjoy childhood while it lasts.

You are probably reading this book because your child is slated to enter kindergarten soon. Maybe you've heard conflicting advice about the best age at which to start. If this is the first of your children to enter formal schooling, you've also got concerns about what the system expects you to have done to prepare him or her.

Will kindergarten be a good experience? Will my son be laughed at or will I be seen as a poor parent if he can't tie his shoe-laces? Can't button his winter jacket? Doesn't know his alphabet?

Is the teacher warm and caring, and will she give my shy daughter the attention she needs? Will kindergarten be just like it was when I was a child, or will it be so different that I won't recognize it, won't approve?

The other day, Bonnie and I were looking at photos we took of our daughter Katharine as she was waiting for the kindergarten bus. It was a scary moment for all of us. We'd car pooled her to preschool, but now there was an enormous yellow bus about to swallow her up at the curb. It only took a few days for both her and us to get used to it, and by the time our son Jonathan came along, we had few anxieties as his big day approached. But the photo of him about to board the bus his first day reveals the same fleeting fears—his and ours. So it really is normal to be anxious, even a little fearful, about this transition.

What concerns us, though, is how little parents know about the kindergartens their children enter. You may rely on neighbors and friends to tell you how to prepare for it, what goes on there, how to identify the best and worst teachers, what the "rules" are. You probably see school as a composite of how you remember it and what your children tell you about their experiences there. Often, you don't have an inkling about the inner workings of a modern elementary school.

Since both of us are educators and consultants, you'll appreciate our view that in general, teachers and administrators should have the primary responsibility for designing and carrying out the curriculum. That's our job, and we should be good at it.

Parents shouldn't be treated as idle bystanders, though. You know your children better than we do. You participate in their education just as much: after all, they spend only two and a half to six hours a day, 180 days a year, with us. The rest of the time they're in your care. You have a right to know what we are doing with your children and why. And finally, which is the point of this book, you have a right to know what your options are.

What's sad about the recent history of public education is that increasingly, parents have been reduced to spectators. Schools educate children according to their best notions of what's appropriate, while you are expected to watch and approve. When school officials tell you your child isn't ready for kindergarten, or for first grade, you are expected to acquiesce. Often, authoritative recommendations affecting a child's whole educational future (such as being retained in grade for an additional year) are communicated in technical language you don't understand. If you want your child placed with a certain teacher, you're often told that placement is random ("picking teachers isn't fair").

If you are to participate in your child's education, you need to know about the educational practices that affect him. That's what this book is all about. We've tried to give you an insider's view of how schools go about teaching kindergarten, what they expect of children at the start and as they move to first grade. You'll see from Chapter 1 that not all programs are alike, and few of them are like the one you attended—unless you went in the past twenty years.

Individual kindergartens have different goals and expectations, and they base their approaches on very different notions about child development. It's important, we think, to know your school's approach. You may decide it's just fine, but if not, you may need to make other plans. But first you need to know your alternatives. Chapter 1 describes three of the most commonly used approaches: traditional, whole language, and developmentally appropriate; and two alternative approaches: Montessori and Waldorf.

Chapter 2 discusses the most important issues you face as your child enters kindergarten. They include:

- Entry age.
- The concept of "readiness."
- Retention.
- Meeting the needs of more advanced and at-risk learners.
- Teacher qualifications.
- Screening and testing.
- Parental involvement.
- Organizational issues such as half- versus full-day kindergarten, class size, and the like.

Not all these issues affect you to the same extent. For example, if your child is an advanced learner you really don't need to worry about the school's policy on retaining children. Since you may want to go right to a particular issue, we've dealt with each one separately. But the issues are linked: entry age is related to retention policy, for example. Therefore, you may want to read the whole chapter to understand the connections.

Chapter 3 covers what you need to know in those last months before your child enters kindergarten and how you can go about finding these things out. We share quite a few insider tips, things you don't usually hear at an open house. And we'll advise you on how to get the information you need without annoying school officials.

Chapter 4 covers what we think you can and should do to prepare your child, regardless of the kind of kindergarten he or she will be going to. We also include some ideas that will be helpful if you know your child is entering a nontraditional program. Remember too that your school may also have specific expectations for incoming students, and if you want your child to have a good start, it'll pay to know what these are and how to prepare for them.

We hope you come away from this book with some solid, practical information you can use to make informed decisions about your child's kindergarten year. The endnotes discuss some additional sources, so that if you want to dig a little deeper you can. We feel that one of the ways we can show our respect for you as a parent and a learner is to share the sources we've used in preparing this book.

Chapter One

All Kindergartens Are Not Alike

Kindergartens in America's schools come in different shapes and sizes, with different goals, purposes, and classroom routines.

Kindergartens came to this country from Europe in the mid-1800s, and at first, very few children attended them. In 1870, there were only twelve in the whole country. Today, over 98 percent of eligible American children are enrolled in kindergarten. The word *kindergarten,* which in German means "a child's garden," was first used by Friederich Froebel in 1837 to describe his program for four- and five-year-olds. Besides coining a new term, he created an entirely new approach to the education of very young children.

In colonial times, young children were considered innately depraved. They were raised in fear and strict discipline; otherwise, the thinking went, there'd be no salvation for them. But Froebel believed children's own feelings and actions should guide their education. Only a few specifics from his program have survived—the practice of "circle" time, large wooden blocks for play, and the name kindergarten—but the idea of child-centeredness has been a guiding principle ever since.

But it's not been the only principle. Not long after the Russians launched Sputnik in 1957, public schools were pressured to raise academic standards. Kindergarten became more closely linked with elementary school and the first-grade curriculum was pushed down into it. The approaches to kindergarten taken over the years spring from different conceptions of early childhood education, have different ideas about what should be accomplished, and conduct the daily routines of teaching in varied ways.

We've identified five kinds of kindergarten: traditional, whole language, developmentally appropriate, Montessori, and Waldorf. We'll describe each of them, examining their underlying beliefs about early childhood education and their goals, curriculum, and typical day.

The Traditional Approach

If you attended public school kindergarten in the United States in the sixties, seventies, and even up through the mid-eighties, you probably experienced a traditional "readiness" program. It's based on the principle that children

- Need to be prepared for first grade.
- Need to master certain "prerequisite" or "readiness" skills for reading and writing (but not reading and writing themselves).
- Have to learn the rituals and routines of a first-grade classroom (sitting quietly, following directions, taking turns).
- Should have time in the day for play.

Central to the readiness philosophy is that children must master certain skills to successfully use their language: listening, speaking, reading, and writing. It's assumed the first two develop at home, but reading and writing are "school" skills. A traditional kindergarten simply prepares children for reading and writing.

The Curriculum
The readiness curriculum includes prereading and prewriting skills, some basic math concepts, social studies, science, music, art, and physical education. Prereading skills include:

- Letter recognition (the ability to identify upper- and lowercase letters).
- Symbol-sound association (when shown the letter *m*, the child correctly makes the "m" sound).
- Rhyming.

2

Some traditional kindergartens also include auditory and visual discrimination. Auditory discrimination is the ability to distinguish between letter sounds (the difference between the sounds "b" and "p"). Visual discrimination is the ability to distinguish between the different shapes of letters (the letter *b* and the letter *p*).

In the traditional approach, children are introduced to a new letter each week through a commercial program designed to teach letters. Some of these programs are comprehensive curriculum materials for teaching reading across the elementary grades (they're called "basal readers"). Other programs, like Alphatime, teach letters and sounds just for kindergartners.

In the weekly approach, the teacher introduces a letter, shows children how it is formed, and explains the sound or sounds it makes. This letter becomes the focus for most of the activities during the week. For example, if it's *p*, children may bring in show-and-tell items beginning with *p*, mark objects beginning with *p* on worksheets and in workbooks, and do things related to the letter (make *p*opcorn or *p*udding; trace, cut, and color *p*igs; have a *p*arade).

Some basal reading series teach letters less directly. For example, the Houghton Mifflin Literature Experience introduces several letters at a time in units that also expose children to literature, writing, dramatic play, and art.

Prewriting skills are things like learning how to hold a pencil properly and forming all the letters of the alphabet. They may also include fine motor control. That's the ability to use the small hand muscles to hold a pencil for writing, drawing, and other tasks. Teachers usually teach prewriting skills through the letter-a-week program. Children practice by tracing the letter, copying it, writing it on worksheets, and coloring predrawn forms.

Basic math concepts include counting objects at least to ten; identifying and sorting numerals, shapes, and money; understanding simple fractions; performing basic addition; recognizing sequences and patterns; and working with size and measurement. Usually the teacher introduces individual concepts to the entire class first and then the children practice and reinforce the skills in workbooks. Some programs teach children basic concepts through math manipulatives (concrete objects)—pennies or buttons instead of objects drawn on a piece of paper.

The social studies curriculum revolves around major holidays and possibly some study units mandated by the district or the state. The concepts are taught through worksheets, books, and projects. The science curriculum usually covers topics like plants, colors, and seasons.

Music is taught through songs and/or dances during group time on the rug. In art, the whole class does projects related to the seasons, holidays, and the social studies and/or science curriculum. Children draw, paint, cut, and paste.

Physical education means one or two sessions a week with the physical education teacher, classroom teacher or simply outside play. Bouncing and catching balls, jumping rope, running, skipping, hopping, and playing games are favorite activities.

If you stepped into a traditional kindergarten classroom, what would you see? An area where children meet for group activities centered around the calendar, songs, and show-and-tell. Tables and chairs (or desks) for every child, a library area, and probably an easel or a space for artwork. Room for dramatic play, often a playhouse. A place to play with large blocks.

A Typical Day
As the children arrive, they sit at tables and do a paper-and-pencil coloring exercise. The teacher gathers everyone on the rug ("circle time") to take attendance, work with the calendar, discuss the weather, sing songs or perform finger plays, and hold show-and-tell. A whole-class lesson introduces or reinforces the letter of the week. Children practice on worksheets and use the letter for follow-up exercises like guessing which items in a "mystery" bag begin with that letter.

Next comes free play, followed by snack time, when children sit at tables and eat together. They help clean up before the teacher reads a story, ushers them outside for a brief play period, and readies them for home.

The Whole Language Approach

This movement started in the early 1980s, although its underpinnings stretch back over a hundred years to the educational philosophers Rousseau and Dewey. Whole language educators believe the following things about how children learn and how literacy should be taught:

- Learning to read and write is as "natural" as learning to speak, provided the same kinds of conditions apply.
- Meaning is the primary goal and purpose of reading, writing, speaking, listening.
- There is no fixed sequence of skills development, and no hierarchy of language skills.
- Materials used to teach literacy should be whole texts that are meaningful and functional.
- Children should have choice and ownership in what they learn: the curriculum should be based on their interests, on what they want to learn and explore.
- Children should learn with others in mixed-ability (heterogeneous) groups as a community of learners.

The Curriculum

A whole language kindergarten focuses primarily on developing literacy, helping children grow as speakers, listeners, readers, and writers. Math, science, social studies, and art are also included. Social interactions are important, but they are tied to literacy and to building a community of learners.

The curriculum is organized around shared reading experiences and "centers." The teacher models reading and writing and engages the children in activities involving big books (large-print books with predictable stories), songs, poems, and chants. In centers scattered around the room, children participate in activities either they, the teacher, or both have designed together. In some classrooms, they sign up for activities, choosing what they want to do; in others, required activities and free choice are mixed. Centers typically include reading, writing, math, science, and art. Play time is also part of every day.

The big difference between this approach and others is the commitment to giving children a say in what they read, write, draw, and learn. For example, the teacher, instead of creating a theme on dinosaurs and planning a series of related activities, allows the children to explore topics that arise from their own questions and concerns. She is guided by their questions, helps them discover answers, and acts as a resource.

Whole language teachers do not "teach" a curriculum. They guide learning by immersing children in literature, modeling literacy strategies, and encouraging them to use their language in meaningful situations. Skills—especially reading and writing—are taught within the context of genuine literacy events such as reading a big book or writing a journal.

A Typical Day

Children settle in by reading a book on their own or to a friend, observing the aquarium, or playing with a puzzle. Then the teacher leads circle time, during which she and the students deal with the day's messages, investigate the calendar, hold show-and-tell, and share books, chants, songs, and poems. Both children's literature and big books (usually with smaller versions for individual children) are used. The teacher introduces new authors, illustrators, and stories and presents reading and writing strategies. Dramatizing the books is a favorite activity.

During center time, the children work in the activity centers of their choice. Centers include reading, writing, math, art, dramatic play, blocks, sand, and listening. In some classrooms, children sign up for the center of their choice and then rotate to others at set intervals. In others, teachers assign students to particular centers and allow them free choice after they've completed their required activities. The day ends with children sharing things they've drawn, written or read, and a final story.

The Developmentally Appropriate Approach

This approach has become popular since the National Association for the Education of Young Children (NAEYC) made it its official policy in the late 1980s. Rather than seeing kindergarten as preparation for first grade, as readiness for literacy, this approach treats kindergarten as an extension of children's preschool activities. It doesn't divide literacy into prereading and reading, prewriting and writing, but instead views literacy as a continuum that starts at birth and continues throughout schooling and beyond.

What does *developmentally appropriate* mean? Simply that what goes on in kindergarten (and in the other grades, too) is appropriate for the children's stage of development. There are several governing principles:

- Children are encouraged to come to kindergarten when they're eligible, not when they're "ready."
- Teachers accept children where they are and take them as far as they can go during the year.
- The curriculum emphasizes growth, not mastery, in four areas: intellectual, social, aesthetic, and physical.
- The curriculum is child-centered, focusing on activities and topics that are inherently appealing to children; children are active participants in their own learning.
- The curriculum is integrated, and the various subject areas are given equal attention.
- Activities are purposeful and genuine; skills are taught in context.
- Children work in a variety of heterogeneous groups, from whole class to small groups to one-on-one.

The Curriculum
The goal of a developmentally appropriate curriculum is to nurture children's intellectual, social, emotional, aesthetic, and physical growth. Literacy, science, social studies, math, music, art, health, and movement are all part of the daily program.

Since there's no beginning or end point in literacy growth, the idea is to accept children where they are in this area and to nurture their emerging abilities. Some may enter kindergarten showing no interest in reading and being unable to identify any letters. Others arrive reading beginning-level books. Some show no interest in writing or drawing, while others avidly draw and write and can even spell some words correctly.

Teachers teach literacy in the context of daily routines, in centers, and in small-group activities. In some programs, instruction is organized around themes and literacy is developed through theme activities. Specific skills such as letters and letter sounds are taught, but the curriculum isn't organized around them.

7

In science, children study the world around them—the seasons, animals, life cycles, plants—through exploration and hands-on activities. In social studies, they learn about getting along together in a community, study the kinds of work done by people in their community, and learn about famous people in history and people from other cultures. Getting along is enhanced through interactions in the classroom, teacher modeling, and solving day-to-day problems.

The math curriculum covers traditional skills such as counting, sorting, recognizing patterns and shapes, graphing, using money, writing the numbers, comparing sets, and measuring. All of these concepts, woven throughout the daily routine, are explored through manipulating objects rather than with paper-and-pencil tasks and rote memorization.

Music and movement are a regular part of a developmentally appropriate kindergarten. Even if the children also have a separate music classroom, songs, finger plays, dance, and movement are incorporated into their classroom routines as well.

In art, children are encouraged to create their own work rather than color in or cut out prepared worksheets or follow specific directions that make all the results look the same.

Physical education, often taught by a specialist in the gymnasium once or twice a week, centers on skills such as bouncing, throwing, and catching balls; running and skipping; basic gymnastics; and relays. Children also spend time outdoors on the playground with the classroom teacher.

A Typical Day

After taking off their coats, putting their attendance cards on the board, and settling in, children choose a classroom activity to pursue until everyone has arrived. Then the teacher gathers everyone on the rug and does the opening exercises—attendance, jobs, calendar, the daily message, and show-and-tell. The children play a major role in each of these activities. The daily message, which is written by the teacher on a large easel pad, not only lets the children know what's happening or reminds them of a special event but also models and teaches beginning reading and writing strategies and skills.

Next, the children engage in music and movement. They learn songs, do finger plays, and act out movements that most likely are related to the current theme. This is followed by "theme time," a large-group activity that involves some discussion of the theme and a read-aloud or shared reading of a trade book or big book related to the theme. After this, the children settle into a ten- to fifteen-minute period of independent reading. As they do so, the teacher circulates among the children, listening to them "read," reading with them, and talking with them about what they're learning.

This is followed by "activity time," a period in which the children engage in small-group activities. Activity time is followed by choice time, when children are free to work or play with anything in the classroom, including the current theme centers as well as blocks, puzzles, and toys. There's also a dramatic play area set up so children can play house, hospital, grocery store and so on. In some developmentally appropriate kindergartens, especially if it's a half-day program, snack time is built into choice time. After cleaning up, the class gathers back on the rug for the closing activity, usually a read-aloud. Then it's time for putting on coats and getting ready for the bus.

The Montessori Approach

The Montessori approach is based on the work of the Italian educator Maria Montessori (1870–1952). The first American Montessori school was established in Tarrytown, New York, in 1911, but the original movement only lasted a few years in the United States. Montessori schools didn't reappear here until the late 1950s, when Nancy Rambusch founded the Whitby School in Connecticut. Today, there are about 4,000 Montessori schools in the United States, of which 150 or so are in public school systems. Most cater to preschool and kindergarten-age children. Many go through third grade, a few through sixth, and just a handful go through the twelfth grade.

There are two main branches of Montessori in the United States. One, represented by the Association Montessori Internationale and headed by surviving Montessori family members, advocates the original Montessori philosophy and practice. The other,

9

represented by members of the American Montessori Society, advocates modernized Montessori approaches. The term *Montessori* isn't copyrighted, so anyone can claim the approach without necessarily having been trained in its methods.

The basic Montessori principles state that children

- Have a remarkable capacity for absorbing information on their own.
- Can literally teach themselves (what Montessori calls "auto-education") with subtle guidance from experienced teachers.
- Need to be respected both as different from adults and from other children. Educating the whole child, and emphasizing children as individuals, is very important.
- Need what Montessori called "liberty"—freedom, within limits, to work and learn on their own, and at their own pace, without adult interference. Giving them time for extended concentration is critical.
- Learn best in a "prepared" environment that provides them with suitable concrete materials and activities to nurture their growth at "sensitive" periods of their development.

In a Montessori school, multisensory learning is very important. The teacher's responsibility is to follow the child's development and to serve the child's needs. Children learn to work together in harmony in a cooperative rather than competitive environment. Multiage classrooms that emulate family learning situations are ideal for promoting this kind of collaborative learning, and many Montessori schools have them.

The Curriculum
The Montessori curriculum is holistic, aiming to nurture each child's intellectual, social, emotional, aesthetic, and physical growth, and covers six major areas:

- The senses. Every aspect of the senses is developed.
- Math. Math is learned primarily through hands-on manipulation of concrete objects.

- Language, both reading and writing. Language study starts with the sounds, then progresses to letters, words, sentences, and paragraphs.
- Practical life. Montessori students learn how to do daily tasks, how to take care of themselves and the environment, good manners.
- Cultural studies—geography, history, zoology, botany, chemistry, and physics.
- Art, music, and movement.

To ensure growth in each of these areas, the Montessori curriculum consists of a prepared environment, Montessori materials, and a facilitative teacher.

The prepared environment is quite striking to a visitor. Everything is at the child's height, giving the room the appearance of a child's workplace rather than an adult classroom inhabited by children. It's predictable and well organized. The Montessori materials are both elaborate and expensive (about $15,000 to equip a single classroom). But as a Montessori educator will quickly point out, the materials themselves are not what's important. It's how they are used by the teachers and the children to promote learning at sensitive periods of a child's development.

The teacher is a keen observer (she has to be, since the lessons and activities are based on daily observations of each child), a skilled presenter of prepared lessons (lessons are taught in very precise language and sequence), and a good mediator. She guides children's progress through the curriculum. The focus is really on the child and his need to learn cognitively and socially. Montessori teachers serve the children, not vice versa. This approach stresses academic learning, but it's equally committed to developing happy, centered, well-rounded children who will continue to learn and to love their fellow human beings.

A Typical Day
Children arrive at school and are greeted at the school door by the teacher. Until everyone arrives, the children work on their own in the classroom. Then they join the teacher on the rug in a circle.

The teacher talks to each child, and each of them tells what activity they'll start the day with.

Children spend the next 90 to 120 minutes doing their "work," using the Montessori materials. This might mean working with a basket of geometric solids, identifying them through touch while blindfolded; sitting at a table reading a simple book (assisted by the teacher); taking turns at a snack table; working with plastic pipes and fittings; drawing and coloring; working with magnets.

During this period, teachers conduct individual lessons or act as mediators in disputes. The children are free to work with any materials in which they have had a lesson, for any amount of time, without adult assistance, if that's their choice. This "work" time is not interrupted.

After lunch and outside play, the three-year-olds go to the nap room to take a nap for the length of time suggested by their parents, while the four- and five-year-olds listen to chapter books while they rest. Children are free to choose another activity if they prefer not to listen to the story.

The bulk of the afternoon is given over to lessons, individually or in small groups, based on what the teachers have observed in the morning and to special activities such as music, art, foreign language, and gym.

The Waldorf Approach

Waldorf schools are few in number (about 550 across the United States), but they have a long history stretching back to Germany in the twenties. Based on the philosophy of Rudolf Steiner (1865–1925), they're the fastest growing nonsectarian educational alternative to public education. As Ronald Kotzsch says:

> To understand it [a Waldorf school], one need grasp some of Steiner's basic ideas: i.e., that the world, and everything in it—stones, stars, trees, animals—has an invisible, spiritual dimension in addition to its visible, material one; that accordingly, the human being has a body, but also a soul (which includes its emotional, artistic and intellectual dimensions) and an eternal, individual spirit; and that the human body, soul and spirit are profoundly interrelated.

The Waldorf approach to kindergarten is based on several of Steiner's principles:

- Education takes place not just in the brain, but throughout the child's body. Sensations, feelings, and imagination are critical pathways to learning.
- The role of the school is to create an environment worthy of the child's unquestioning imitation of adults.
- Reading and writing instruction belong in first grade, not kindergarten.
- The teacher, not a textbook, is the source for the curriculum.

The Curriculum

The Waldorf kindergarten is different from other grades in that it does not directly teach reading, writing, math, or subject areas. Rather, it focuses on the development of children's imagination and self-reliance and exposes them to the natural world. Emphasis is on the rhythm of the year in nature (the seasons); the arts (movement, painting, sewing, sculpting); and traditional festivals (Easter, Thanksgiving, the Feast of St. Nicholas, Harvest, May Day). These things are explored through songs, movement, play, and stories told by the teacher.

A visitor notices right away that the Waldorf kindergarten is different. Because children absorb everything around them, every effort is made to make the classroom beautiful. The classroom is painted in pastel colors and draped with pastel fabrics. Only natural materials like beeswax crayons, cut logs, and cloth dolls are used. Modern media and commercial materials are discouraged both in school and at home.

The teacher plays a critical role here, choosing and directing activities and modeling the qualities she seeks to develop. For example, she tells, rather than reads, stories, allowing children to use their imagination to the fullest extent so they can create their own pictures in their minds.

Free play of the child's imagination is important. Children have time each day to play with anything in the classroom—cloth dolls (without complete faces, so they can create characters of their own choosing), kitchen items, small movable wooden frames draped with cloth, pillows, baskets, cut logs, pine cones.

The children are responsible for daily tasks such as setting up and preparing snacks, which follow a predictable pattern. Children help prepare these snacks, kneading the dough and cutting the vegetables, setting the table and clearing up. Seeing and participating in a process from start to finish is an important part of the approach. These daily tasks, done together, help children's development in all areas.

Although reading and writing are not formally taught, children are prepared for literacy in a number of ways. Teachers try to instill a love of learning and the will to do what needs to be done for their own sakes by modeling these attributes. They expose children to songs, stories, and verse that provide them with important literary and cultural knowledge.

Science and social studies are woven into the daily routines. The emphasis is on natural science, and children observe changes in nature by doing things like bringing a monarch caterpillar into the classroom, watching its metamorphosis, and then setting it free; gardening; and baking bread. Social learning centers primarily on the rhythm of the year and on festivals and is conveyed mostly through stories and hands-on participation. For example, children learn about autumn, harvesting, Halloween, and Thanksgiving. They celebrate Easter, St. Nicholas Day, Channukah, Christmas, and May Day.

Math is not formally taught either, but many of the songs and verses involve counting, as do many of the daily tasks, and children learn simple counting through them.

A Typical Day

Until all the children have arrived, everyone plays outside. When they come in, they hang up their coats and are greeted personally by the teacher one at a time. They wash their hands (a bowl and hand towels are set out on a table) and come to the circle on the rug. They start each day with "morning verses," in which they greet the sun and each other and perform rhythmic games or finger plays; a short nature story may be told. Then they do a whole-class morning activity. On Mondays, they paint (using only red, blue, and yellow paints). On Tuesdays, Wednesdays, and Thursdays, they color (using red, blue, and yellow beeswax crayons). On Fridays, they do beeswax modeling. After cleaning up, the children engage in free play and prepare the snack. After the snack area is cleaned up, a transitional song leads them to rest. This is followed by another circle time involving verses and songs. Next they eat the snack they prepared earlier and then play outside. After this, they gather in a circle for the final story of the day and are then ready for dismissal.

Some Closing Comments

While the kindergartens we've looked at have different views about children's learning, different goals for early childhood education, and different beliefs about the best ways to teach young children, there are some similarities.

Whole language and developmentally appropriate kindergartens have a lot in common, although whole language originates in literacy education, the developmentally appropriate approach in early childhood education. Both are committed to fitting the curriculum to the child rather than the other way around, and both emphasize children's ownership and choice in what they do in the classroom. Recently, however, early childhood educators in this country are being influenced by Reggio Emilia, a community in Italy with a unique approach to educating young children that includes a balance between child-centered and teacher-centered activities. It's also the case that many traditional kindergartens have recently begun to adopt routines usually found in whole language or developmentally appropriate programs—things like big books, music and movement, and centers.

But many differences remain. Whole language and developmentally appropriate programs emphasize literature more than the others do. Literature is not a major focus of a traditional program and plays only a minor role in a Montessori classroom; Waldorf kindergartens exclude reading literature all together and focus on storytelling.

The various approaches have striking differences when it comes to dramatic play. Imaginative play is discouraged in a Montessori approach—instead, children interact with concrete objects. A Waldorf school, on the other hand, places enormous stress on imaginative play. Traditional, whole language, and developmentally appropriate kindergartens include it, but not to the extent that Waldorf ones do.

There's also a big difference in the way these kindergartens teach reading and writing. Montessori has the most detailed and comprehensive scheme—nothing is left to chance in a program that starts with sounds, then builds to letters, words, sentences, and paragraphs. Traditional kindergartens don't teach "real" reading and writing, but they do teach reading and writing "readiness" skills. Whole language and developmentally appropriate kindergartens introduce children to reading through literature and to composing through actual writing, but they don't teach skills in isolation or base their literacy curriculum on letters. Waldorf schools, on the other hand, pretty much leave the teaching of reading and writing to first grade and beyond.

If you use our descriptions to identify what's going on in your school, we'd offer this caution. Just because a program calls itself one thing or another doesn't mean it will look exactly like the ones we've described above. Public schools have no nationwide system of certification for kindergarten teachers or training in specific approaches, so you'll always have to look beyond the labels and determine for yourself which approach is being used.

Because their preservice training is often haphazard or even nonexistent, many kindergarten teachers don't have a recognizable approach, but instead use whatever they find works in their classroom. Their eclectic way of teaching might not resemble anything we've described here.

Expect to find quite a bit of variation within a particular approach as well as between approaches. Traditional kindergartens will vary the most because they are currently in transition, and many of them have been influenced by whole language and developmentally appropriate philosophies. Waldorf and Montessori kindergartens are likely to be the most consistent, because they both stem from well-defined philosophies and insist their teachers be properly trained. (Be careful, though, to check whether the teachers at the Montessori school you might be considering for your child are in fact Montessori-trained. A school can call itself Montessori without having a Montessori-trained faculty.)

16

Is there a right way to teach kindergarten? Is one of these approaches better than the others? What's "right" or "better" really depends on your view of how children can best be taught and whose educational philosophy you find most compatible with your own beliefs. If you see kindergarten as a place where children need to be taught readiness skills primarily through worksheets and workbooks, then you'll be drawn to a traditional approach. If you see kindergarten as a child-centered place where teachers accept children at their stage of development and nurture their emerging abilities in all areas, then you'll be drawn to whole language or developmentally appropriate approaches. If you find yourself attracted to the educational philosophies of Maria Montessori or Rudolph Steiner, then the kindergartens based on those philosophies will be right for you. Even though we have developed our own kindergarten program, we think you should advocate whichever one you believe is best for you and your child. While we have concerns about the basis for a strictly traditional kindergarten (it rests on assumptions about child language development that are no longer widely held in the field), we see the other approaches as representing legitimately different beliefs about what's important for five- and six-year-olds to experience in these formative years.

Of course, if your belief system lies outside these approaches—for example, you subscribe to a strictly religious view of early childhood education, or you believe that children should be taught only by their parents—then you won't find what you're looking for here. In that case, you'll have to look for private schools whose philosophy is compatible with yours, or home-school your kindergartner.

Chapter Two

Kindergarten Issues

If sending your child to kindergarten were just a matter of registering her and putting her on a bus at the beginning of the year, why worry? But it isn't that simple. Depending on your child's age, preschool experience, abilities and interests, and personality, there are important things you need to know before you enroll her and during the time she's there.

We discuss most of them here, but you may want to concentrate on the ones that seem most relevant to your situation. However, since some issues affect and are affected by others, we've cross-referenced sections we think have special bearing. We've included answers to some frequently asked questions, and occasionally we include a story about how an issue has played out in real life.

Some of the terms used in this book might be unfamiliar to you, so here they are, and how we define them. Unfortunately, these terms are sometimes used differently by educators, and so you will always need to find out how they are defined in your situation:

Term	How We Define It
Preschool	Any educational experience provided to children before they become eligible for kindergarten (it includes private nursery schools, and publicly funded programs

such as Headstart and preschools for children with special needs). Preschool does not add any years to a child's formal education.

Holding Out	The practice of parents choosing not to send the child to kindergarten when he or she is chronologically eligible. Holding out a child either involves repeating four-year-old preschool, or attending a private pre-kindergarten program, or keeping the child at home. Holding out a child delays entrance to the child's formal schooling.
Pre-Kindergarten/ Developmental Kindergarten (these terms are used synonymously)	An educational program (publicly or privately funded, and situated either in a preschool or in an elementary school) for children chronologically eligible for kindergarten who are considered developmentally not ready. Typically, a child attending a Pre-K or Developmental Kindergarten will go to a regular kindergarten afterwards. This program adds a year to the child's formal schooling.
Pre-First/Transitional First (these terms are used synonymously)	A grade (in elementary school) sandwiched in between kindergarten and first grade for children who are considered de velopmentally not ready for first grade. Typically, a child will go from this program into a regular first grade. This program adds a year to the child's formal schooling.

19

Entry Age

In most states, children are eligible for kindergarten between the ages of four and six; most schools require they turn five during their kindergarten year. But when to start isn't as simple as it sounds.

First of all, schools almost always set an entry cut-off date—a child needs to have turned five before that date to qualify for kindergarten that year. In most states, the cut-off date is in the late fall or early winter.

The entry date itself isn't that important. What matters is how close a child's birthday is to it. For example, if the cut-off date is December 31 and Tucker was born on December 30, he'll still be four when he starts school and probably be the youngest in the class. On the other hand, Colleen, born on January 1, just two days later, will have to wait until the following year to start school. That means some kindergartners may be almost a full year older than others, even though everyone entered kindergarten according to the rules.

So there will be a wide distribution of abilities in class, even if all parents send their children on schedule. But they don't. Some, fearing their children will be retained in kindergarten, hold them back for a year so they'll stand a better chance of progressing normally through the grades. Others, desperately wanting their children to excel from the start, hold them back so they'll be a year older (and presumably more likely to excel) when they start kindergarten.

Then there are the parents who figure that if everyone else is holding out their children, they'd better, too. Why risk having the youngest child in kindergarten? When many parents keep their children back, for whatever reasons, the disparities in ages get wider and wider.

Therefore, you need to know not only the official policy, but also the actual entry age in your school district. Are school officials or teachers recommending that parents of "young" five-year-olds hold their children out for another year? It makes a big difference if they're actively welcoming all five-year-olds or discouraging younger ones from entering on time. You may be able to learn the average age of kindergartners from previous years, but in most schools, there's so much variation from year to year this won't help much. The figures you really need are *this* year's, but they will be much harder to obtain, since all the children probably aren't yet enrolled and the school may be reluctant to release the information in any case.

Does it matter if a child is a "young" kindergartner? All things being equal, most children who meet the cut-off date will progress normally through the grades, and most of the differences between "older" and "younger" children will have evened out by about fourth grade. But things aren't always equal. If teachers routinely recommend that the lowest-achieving children repeat kindergarten or assign them to transitional or pre-first programs, or if the curriculum is not adapted to the child, then "younger" kindergartners are much more likely to be retained.

In a recent article, Sharon Kagan proposes a good solution to the age issue:

> We need to homogenize the entry standards so that all children—regardless of income, language, or gender—enter school at a given chronological time, then we need to individualize services to match the children's needs after entry. In this way the vast majority of the nation's kindergarten children will enter developmentally appropriate kindergartens at the age-appropriate time.

But we have to admit that some children are "young" developmentally even though they may not be that young chronologically. To send such children to kindergarten, even to a developmentally appropriate program, "on schedule" is not an easy decision. Sending or holding out a developmentally young child is a decision that will take very careful deliberation by his parents and other caregivers, the preschool staff, and his pediatrician.

My son Tolon has a November birthday and is very active. He's eligible to start kindergarten in my district. Should I send him?
If Tolon has been attending preschool, ask his teacher there for advice. Find out how well the kindergarten teachers accept active children. Will Tolon be expected to sit in a seat for long periods and do things that are hard at his stage of development? Active

21

boys are, regrettably, retained more often than their classmates. But if the teachers are accepting, and if Tolon is progressing normally in other areas, then there's absolutely no reason to hold him out. He won't be the first or last active young boy in kindergarten.

My daughter Rachel was late learning to talk and seems to have little interest in "print." Should I wait a year to send her to kindergarten?
Rachel might have a learning delay or (even less likely) a learning disability, but it's too early to say. She may just be a late bloomer who'll catch up in a year or so. If the kindergarten adapts its curriculum to children's needs, then Rachel should be there. If she does develop learning difficulties, she'll receive appropriate early intervention. However, if the school has a traditional program and you've already sensed it will recommend that Rachel not enter, or will probably retain her the next year if she does, she may be better off going to a developmentally appropriate preschool for another year.

What is the best cut-off date?
Any date from late summer to the end of December is fine. We think it's time for parents and schools to agree on a couple of things. Parents should send their children to school on time, and kindergartens should adapt their programs to the children who enroll. The rest of the primary grades, too, need to follow along. That way parents wouldn't have to guess about when to send their children, and schools could concentrate on providing appropriate experiences for children rather than creating makeshift arrangements for those who aren't quite "ready."

Michael's story

Sue and Jack Ronaldson decided to place their only son Michael in a private pre-K program for a year rather than send him to kindergarten on time. According to Sue, Michael is very active and is tall for his age. She didn't think he could stay focused—even though he was bright enough—and worried that he might be incapable of handling behavior expectations and interacting with other children.

22

Sue and Jack's other concern was one of the teachers Michael might get. "I spoke to a number of parents," Sue told us, "and they related how their children—especially the young boys—were treated by this teacher. She'd almost certainly ostracize Michael, and I was concerned his first year might start on a wrong note. This teacher had a reputation for yelling at the children, which isn't what I wanted for Michael."

So Sue and Jack enrolled Michael in a developmentally appropriate pre-K program, and now, a year later, he's ready for kindergarten. Sue is much more confident that Michael will be able to cope, even if he is assigned to the teacher others had warned her about. "Maturity-wise, by going to the preschool, he's learned about how to maneuver in a building with multiple classrooms. He knows about being in a room with twenty people and he understands what it is to go to school without me. The curriculum in the pre-K program was more like kindergarten than preschool. He was successful at it and I think he's ready for kindergarten now."

Sue and Jack still have some concerns, but they're the usual ones about getting on the bus and being able to cope in the world of a big school.

Readiness

What does it mean that a child is "ready" for kindergarten or "ready" for first grade? Different things to different people. In the early 1900s, Arnold Gesell said that a child's mental abilities unfold according to a natural timetable and that a child shouldn't be taught to read until he or she is ready. This definition rests on the premise that there are critical developmental stages before which certain things cannot be done. The argument goes: you can't hurry nature along, and it's futile to try.

Another view also comes from the early 1900s. William S. Gray argued that reading consists of readiness skills, which belong in kindergarten, and actual reading, which belongs in first grade. Kindergarten prepares children for reading; first grade teaches it. This idea soon expanded to include writing readiness (learning the letters, holding a pencil) versus actual writing, again divided between kindergarten and first grade. Eventually, the notion that kindergarten should prepare children for first grade (not just in reading and writing, but in behavior too) took hold and has guided traditional kindergartens ever since.

Neither of these notions of readiness has stood the test of time. Yet Gesell's followers still actively promote his ideas, and Gray's distinction between prereading and reading skills still forms the basis of many traditional programs.

In the past twenty years, we've come to see the development of a child's literacy abilities in terms of a steady progression of listening, speaking, reading, and writing abilities that span several years. We call this progression *emergent literacy*. Emergent literacy can't be neatly divided into separate and distinct stages. As Leslie Mandel Morrow puts it:

> The concept of emergent literacy suggests that one does not suddenly learn to read; rather, becoming literate is a process that begins at birth and continues throughout one's lifetime . . . Stages in reading development are not as precise as we might like them to be. Certain traits do seem to be acquired by many youngsters before others, but the dividing lines among traits and among youngsters are not always distinct. Different children pass through stages at different levels of maturity . . . We must not be trapped into believing that all children must pass through all stages or all at the same time and in the same order . . . We must never presume that the stages are fixed, or that a child cannot operate at a "later" stage before an "earlier" one. (p. 80)

We are now coming to understand that a child's mental abilities unfold partly because of his internal development (nature) and partly because of his experiences in the real world (nurture). Both are necessary ingredients for growth. Slowly but surely, traditional kindergartens are beginning to let go of "readiness," but the transition is taking a long time. Your child's school may still be clinging to it. Developmentally appropriate and whole language kindergartens are both based on the concept of emergent literacy,

24

recognizing that it's more important for the school to be ready for the child than the child to be ready for the school.

I keep hearing about giving children "the gift of time." What is this, and what's the purpose of it?
We've already mentioned Arnold Gesell, who early on suggested that a child should reach a certain stage of mental maturity before being taught reading and writing. His followers argue that children who are mentally "immature" should attend a pre-kindergarten or pre-first program to get an extra year in which their mental abilities can catch up. Hence the "gift of time." Perhaps as many as half of all schools provide this extra year for children they don't think are "ready."

We disagree. Children need appropriate activities in the program they're in, not an extra year to catch up. This so-called gift of time is actually a form of retention, and there's no credible evidence that it has any positive long-term benefits. But this isn't to say that no child, under any circumstances, will benefit from spending an additional year in a program appropriate to her needs. The trouble with every rule is that there are always exceptions.

I thought one of the national goals for education was that all children come to school "ready to learn." Doesn't that conflict with what you've just been saying?
On the surface, it does. It's unfortunate that the framers of the national goals chose the word *ready* here, and they've received quite a bit of criticism in the professional literature since then. The real intent, in our opinion, is to commit more resources to preschool education, especially to disadvantaged children, to better meet their needs for appropriate learning before they come to school.

We think all children are "ready to learn." The real question is whether they're ready to learn a curriculum that's inappropriate to their needs. Some see the readiness goal as another sign of pushing the first-grade curriculum down into kindergarten and the kindergarten curriculum down into preschool.

Although we're not sure what the real motives are (and as we write this, the national goals are under renewed scrutiny), but anything that better funds and supports appropriate programs for all preschoolers gets our vote.

What if my child's preschool teacher says my child isn't ready for kindergarten, but I say he is? Or vice versa?
There's no easy answer to this tough question (see Amy's story, below). If the teacher understands your child and the particular program, then listen carefully to what she's recommending. She may be saying your child isn't ready for the school's approach. But your child may be more than ready for a different one.

If neither she nor you knows much about the kindergarten, consult several people (friends who have had children in the school, kindergarten teachers, the school principal) and see what they recommend. But remember that in the end, it's your call.

My daughter Haley is very shy. I took her to the school screening in April, and they said she wasn't ready to enter kindergarten. What should I do?
Such an important decision shouldn't be based just on a short session with someone Haley doesn't know and may not even be comfortable with (see also Screening Before Kindergarten, p. 47). If she's been in preschool, if her teachers there have no reservations about her, and if you feel she's ready, then send her. Her shyness is part of her personality and doesn't necessarily reflect her developmental level or abilities.

Mention Haley's shyness to the kindergarten teacher so she can make a special effort to include Haley in activities and provide a little extra TLC. You may even want to talk to the school principal ahead of time to try to make sure Haley is assigned to a teacher who is particularly sensitive to shy children. But most teachers, regardless of their philosophy, are very good with shy children and will take Haley under their wing.

I think schools should be ready for children, not the other way around. But in the orientation session, the message was clear: your child needs to be ready for kindergarten.

Don't panic. Your child, like most children, probably *is* ready, and while the program may not be quite what you're looking for, she will most likely have a happy and successful year. But if she's "young," then you do need to think about the issues we discuss in this chapter, because she's more likely to have problems in a kindergarten that stresses "readiness" than in one that takes a developmentally appropriate approach. If you really feel that neither you nor your child can handle this situation, explore other possibilities. Private school is one of them. Holding your child out for a year and providing her with a good preschool program is another. Home-schooling is also an option.

Amy's story

Evelyn and Thomas Rodino's child, Amy, is currently in first grade. She wouldn't be if Evelyn and Tom had followed the advice of her preschool teacher.

Amy was a biter as a toddler—she chewed people and things—and Evelyn feels bad because she used to yell at her a lot. She thinks this might have been why Amy was so quiet and "pulled back." Amy went to preschool as a three-year-old, where everything went well except that she shadowed the teacher and was very quiet around other children. Part of the problem, it turned out, was that Amy couldn't hear properly. Once she had tubes put in her ears, she became more active and involved.

In the four-year-old preschool class, Amy was still very much attached to the teacher and had difficulty engaging in activities on her own. The teacher recommended against kindergarten, believing that Amy would have a hard time on her own and that the teacher would probably not give Amy the individual attention she needed.

Evelyn and Tom really weren't sure what to do. As Evelyn recalls: "We understood what her preschool teacher was saying, and we agreed. We were there. We saw Amy following her around like a puppy dog. But I think she needed a push to get away from it. I went to the kindergarten orientation, and came away from there feeling that there are a lot of different kinds of kids going to kindergarten, and they're not all perfect kindergarten kids. I didn't think Amy was perfect either, but I felt she'd set up this precedent for the way she was supposed to be around her preschool teacher, and that's the way she was with her, and I didn't feel that spending a third year with the same person was really going to help. It was a hard push, but I felt she needed to go on."

So Evelyn and Tom sent Amy to kindergarten. At first Evelyn wasn't sure they'd made the right decision. "One of the things Amy complained about was being handed from one unfamiliar adult to another. She didn't like getting on the morning bus with a bus driver she didn't know, being ushered off by an aide she didn't know—and not always the same one—and being taken to her kindergarten teacher. All she could say about library or gym was that the teacher left her there! She was uncomfortable, I would say, for a good month or so, I could feel it from her. She never cried about getting on the bus, she never worried about going to school, but I knew she was anxious. Sometimes she'd say to me, 'Do you think the same person will get me off the bus? Do you think I'm going to have the same bus driver?' We got to know the bus drivers by name, so we could relate to them on a personal level.

"But she did it! She had a great kindergarten year. She grew by leaps and bounds. Her report card does say how at times she still has a problem going on to the next activity at center time, and she still likes to check in to show the teacher what's she's done. But she's become very social. And she's been participating in activities on her own—camping, swimming lessons, skiing lessons, ice-skating lessons. And she does all these things well. I don't see the clingyness any more."

After thinking about it, we realized that from the preschool teacher's point of view, Amy really wasn't ready for kindergarten. Indeed, if Amy hadn't been assigned to a very caring teacher she might well have had a very difficult year. Evelyn was right to trust her own judgment and look beyond Amy's clinging behavior to what she really needed, which was a change of teacher and program. Amy probably will always be on the shy side, but academically she's fine, and so far she's well able to handle the first-grade curriculum.

Retention

Retention "in grade" means repeating kindergarten with the same or a different teacher. But it also comes in a couple of disguises: a prekindergarten program (often called a "developmental" kindergarten to distinguish it from a preschool program) and a prefirst or "transitional" year between kindergarten and first grade (the child goes from this class into first grade). Although schools often claim they aren't retaining children by assigning them to these kinds of programs, they are. Anything that adds an extra year to a child's schooling is a form of retention.

Retention is still very common, although it's declining somewhat from a peak in the 1980s. A 1992 survey by May and Kundert found that 57 percent of the New York State schools responding operated prefirst programs. Also, while some schools never make children repeat kindergarten, others retain as many as 40 percent (Allington and McGill-Franzen, 1995).

It may surprise you—it certainly surprises teachers who routinely retain children—to learn that it doesn't work. While it adds a year to a child's schooling, it provides few if any benefits for the child. Recent studies show unequivocally that children retained in grade do no better academically or socially than children allowed to go forward with their peers. Worse, they drop out of school more frequently. And the situation is no better with prefirst or transitional programs. According to researchers, children in these programs show little or no improvement compared to children who progress through first grade on schedule. But their self-concept and socioemotional development are often negatively affected, whether they were sent to these programs for academic or social reasons.

Given that an extra year in school costs an average of four thousand dollars per child, retention is also an expensive option—it costs public schools about ten billion dollars a year nationwide, according to researchers Shepard and Smith. That's an awful lot of taxpayer money down the drain for something that doesn't work.

Parents and teachers tend to look only at the short-term results of keeping a child back. Retained children do seem to do better in the second year in the same grade. But compared with their peers, they are already slipping behind. And over the span of elementary and secondary school, they are no better off. For children who are not progressing within the normal limits of individual differences, the greater harm of retention is that if their educational needs are not met in these critical years, they may never catch up. Allowing them to "wait" in watered-down programs rather than addressing their educational needs is worse than promoting them to another grade that educators don't think they are "ready" for.

Here's what we recommend:

- If you haven't noticed anything particularly unusual in your child's development, or even if there have been some concerns (delays in learning to speak, coordination difficulties, lack of interest in "print," and so on) expect he will attend kindergarten and then go to first grade on schedule. Challenge any suggestion to the contrary.

- If someone recommends your child be placed in a transitional class or be retained, don't accept the recommendation without carefully examining the reasons offered and the evidence provided. Never act on the basis of one person's recommendation or a single test. Only allow your child to be retained or placed in a transitional program under the most extraordinary circumstances and after full consultation with everyone involved. And if your gut feeling is that it isn't right, it probably isn't.

- If you have to decide between holding your child out before kindergarten or allowing him to attend a transitional class or be retained, hold him out. Once a child has started school, there are negative effects associated with being retained or placed in a transitional class. An appropriate preschool is a better alternative, with one caution. A recent study (May, Kundert, and Brent, 1995) has indicated that students who started school late are at higher risk of being placed in special education programs than students who entered on time. They weren't at higher risk of being retained, though.

- If your child has learning or other difficulties, these problems should first be addressed within the regular classroom. If that isn't sufficient, get individual help from qualified specialists. Retention or a transitional class should always be a strategy of last resort.

Have you ever recommended a child be retained?
In the ten years that Bonnie has been teaching kindergarten, she's retained just two children (out of roughly 350). Both had November birthdays, one boy and one girl. The girl was shy and suffered tremendously from separation anxiety throughout the first year of kindergarten. The boy was having trouble learning. Since he was quite young, it was difficult to determine whether he just wasn't there yet, developmentally, or if he in fact did have a learning disability. In both cases, the retention decision came after all aspects of the situation were examined, including how the children would fare in first grade, their self-esteem, and the prospects for a successful second year. It's very important that children not be made to think they've failed or that they're being "punished" for poor performance. It's also critical that parents play a major role in the decision.

There's one other situation in which we think it might be appropriate to consider retention, and that's the combination of a very immature child and a very rigid, traditional first grade.

My district retains about 20 percent of the children in kindergarten, and has prefirst classrooms in all its elementary schools. Is there anything I can do to change this?
If you bring this issue to the attention of the elementary school principals and teachers and to the school board, you can make a difference. Retention practices may not change in time for your child, but they may for other children or later siblings. We suggest several strategies:

- Point out the negative effects of retention (Shepard and Smith's book *Flunking Grades* is one of the most persuasive we know). This research may come as quite a surprise to educators in your district.
- Encourage the school district to examine the effects of its own practices (Allington and McGill-Franzen's chapter in

the book *No Quick Fix* suggests some excellent strategies for accomplishing this). They'll almost certainly find out how ineffective they are.

- Show the school board how expensive retention is, especially if the long-term effects are negligible. Your district may not be happy about losing these programs, but saving taxpayers' money will resonate with them. And remember: if a school has a prefirst program, it may try to fill it, even if that means assigning children who may not belong there.

John's story

Jane and Paul Mattson's son John was doing fine in kindergarten, as far as they knew. He'd had an uneventful preschool, and for the first ten weeks of kindergarten there were no signs of trouble. But at a January meeting, John's teacher began getting all excited about his handwriting. According to Jane: "The real issue was that he couldn't make clear letters, and he couldn't keep them on a line. The school wanted to start physical therapy right away, but in order to get it, John had to be labeled as having some sort of disability. We were very concerned about the labeling process and having this label follow him all through school."

So Jane and Paul consulted the director of an early childhood program at a local college. The director thought the school was making a mountain out of a molehill and recommended an outside evaluation of John's difficulties. A specialist told them that John did have muscle problems in his shoulder. These could be treated aggressively, which might help him or not, but if left untreated, the problem would take care of itself in a couple of years. Based on this evaluation, the Mattsons decided to hire a private occupational therapist to work with John.

Jane recalls a subsequent meeting at the school. "We had this absolutely startling conference where the special education director talked about John going on to first grade and his handwriting being so bad that he wouldn't be able to line up numbers to do arithmetic and this would ruin his academic

career! Well, as it turns out, John still doesn't line up num-
bers but it doesn't make any difference because he does all
his math in his head!"

    The school said that if the Mattsons didn't allow John to be
placed in a school physical therapy program in first grade, they
would place him in prefirst instead. The Mattsons considered
private school, but in the end decided not to fight the district.
John was evaluated and labeled, placed in first grade, and
assigned to a physical therapist. As Paul described it, "All he
had was a half hour of physical therapy a week. John went to
this special room, they threw balls to him and he practiced
writing big letters."

    How is John doing now? He's in eighth grade, all honors
classes, carrying a well-above-ninety average. And how's his
handwriting? Still awful. "In accelerated math," Jane recalls,
"the teacher gives the students a graphing problem and insists
on it being done with paper and pencil—except John, of
course. He's allowed to do it on the computer!"

    But John seems to have developed a permanent phobia
about handwriting. Jane and Paul really don't know if his
muscular problems have gone away, but he cannot and will
not handwrite anything. Luckily, his teachers now see
beyond this to his fine mind, and so his difficulties with pen-
manship really aren't getting in the way of his academic
progress.

Meeting the Needs of More Advanced Learners

All parents expect their child's needs to be met, but parents of
children whose development before school seems to have been
unusually rapid have their own particular concerns. How will the
kindergarten treat a child who already knows how to read and
write? Or has genuine talent in math, music, or art?

    No school is willing to admit publicly that it can't meet the
needs of advanced children. Most proudly proclaim they challenge
every child to his or her full potential. But the truth is that most
elementary schools—especially those with fixed curriculums (the
same for everyone, with the expectation that everyone will master

it)—do have difficulties with children at the upper end of the spectrum. If your child is an advanced learner, you should know some details about the school's plans to meet these special needs.

One concern is the child might be bored, which certainly doesn't set a good tone for the beginning of formal education. Do school officials recommend bypassing kindergarten and enrolling your child directly in first grade? Do they intend to send her to another grade for instruction in her strong areas? Do they offer a supplementary, pullout program for "gifted and talented" children? Or do they meet these needs within the kindergarten program?

The approach is usually related to the kindergarten's philosophy. Traditional programs don't easily accommodate very advanced children. They may recommend instead promotion to first grade, enrollment in a "gifted and talented" program, or participation in another grade level's reading, writing, or content-area program.

Developmentally appropriate programs can accommodate advanced children better because they don't establish upper or lower limits to growth and the curriculum adjusts to where children are in their development. Just because a program is labeled developmentally appropriate, though, doesn't mean it will automatically challenge the more advanced students. But in theory, it should, and we know many programs that do.

However, some parents overestimate their child's abilities, either because they have unrealistically high expectations for them or because they haven't had broad enough experiences with children to know where, on the continuum, their own child lies. These parents sometimes find it hard to accept that their child's abilities, though in the upper end of the normal range, are not exceptional. On the other hand, teachers sometimes underestimate children. They're unaware of their genuine talent because they never ask them to share what they know or give them a chance to show what they can do.

For these reasons, we think you should tell the school about your child's special capabilities at registration or orientation. Show teachers examples of your child's talents and explain his unusual strengths.

Recently, a parent came to the orientation at Bonnie's school and talked to her about her daughter. She was already reading and writing stories, played with older children, and generally acted older than her age. Bonnie and the parent agreed that the daughter should enter kindergarten rather than go to first grade. But by December, Bonnie and the parent agreed that the child would be better off in first grade, and she was switched there.

My child Shea is entering kindergarten this fall, and he already can read and write at a first-grade level. Some of my friends say he should skip kindergarten and go straight into first grade. What do you think?
There are always a few children who come to kindergarten already reading and writing, so Shea may not be all that exceptional. There will probably be other children at the same level. We'd recommend you send Shea to kindergarten. After all, he's still a five-year-old with many of the same intellectual, social, and emotional needs as other kindergartners, regardless of his advanced literacy abilities. On rare occasions, a child may spend a few months in kindergarten, and then everyone agrees it's right to promote him or her to first grade. But we'd still recommend an initial placement in kindergarten.

Kimmy is already showing signs of giftedness in art. Is there anything I should be doing?
That reminds us of the kindergarten experiences of two well-known children's authors/illustrators, Eric Carle and Tomie de Paola. Eric's teacher recognized his extraordinary artistic abilities, allowed him to explore them freely, and advised his parents to nurture his talent. Tomie's teachers discouraged his abilities at school, although he was supported at home by his parents. They've both turned out to be enormously successful artists, so maybe true talent prevails, whether it's encouraged or repressed.

If Kimmy's talents aren't encouraged in school, then support them at home. It may be unrealistic to expect schools to provide the level of instruction a truly gifted child artist or musician needs, but they should nurture and celebrate this talent. Many kindergarten teachers do.

My school doesn't provide a "gifted and talented" program for kindergartners, only for children in grades three and beyond. Should they?

If by a "gifted and talented" program you mean one in which children are pulled out to work on special projects with other "bright" children, then we don't recommend it for kindergartners (or for anyone else, for that matter). Children should be challenged daily within the classroom. This isn't easy, we admit, and there are limits to what one teacher can do.

But if such a program is the only challenging moment in a child's week, then it's better than not being challenged at all. Remember that a pullout program will only occupy a fraction of a child's school time, so at best it's a Band-Aid solution. And there's no guarantee such a program will genuinely challenge your child. It might just involve more worksheets!

Meeting the Needs of At-risk Children

One of the biggest challenges parents and early childhood educators face is predicting whether a child will have learning or other difficulties in school. Predictions are difficult for a couple of reasons.

Normally developing children often exhibit the same symptoms as children who aren't on schedule, and children "grow out of" some of their difficulties without any intervention. But how do you tell which are part of normal development, which a child will grow out of, and which need attention to prevent them from failure?

For example, a child who reverses his letters or numbers (reading *b* for *d*, or writing *b* for *d*) could either be showing signs of a learning disability or simply making temporary errors on his way to mastering these skills. The problem could go away without any help (the reversals are just part of normal development); it could take quite a while before it corrects itself, with minimal or no intervention (the child will outgrow these errors); or it could persist into the primary grades (the child's development is seriously delayed or he has a learning difficulty). At what point do we say these reversals are evidence of a learning difficulty? A premature diagnosis may falsely label a normal child. Wait too long and the genuine needs of a child at risk of failure will be ignored.

The truth is we can't accurately pinpoint the signs of a child at risk before he's started school. We rely on careful observation, intuition, and professional judgment to determine the best course of action for one who appears to be having difficulties or who we think will likely have them later on. Almost always, the combined wisdom of parents and teachers will be the most valuable guide for action. But we do have some suggestions:

- Be concerned about your child between the ages of two and five if her language learning difficulties seem to persist beyond a reasonable time. There is enormous variation in all aspects of children's development, but if you see she doesn't seem to be growing in particular areas or has difficulties that don't go away on their own, then you should probably seek help. Consult your pediatrician first, who may lead you to specialists. Some severe disabilities may require intensive and prolonged attention that should begin well before kindergarten.
- Even if your child has legitimate developmental difficulties, enroll him in kindergarten on schedule. Public schools must adapt their programs to include children with difficulties and provide appropriate and timely assistance to meet their needs. Most will offer *prereferral intervention,* which means arranging for help without labeling the child a "special education" student. We don't recommend a transitional class for the reasons we gave earlier. But don't let a child with difficulties stay at home without getting help.
- If you are suddenly confronted at a parent-teacher conference in May with the news that your child has difficulties that you knew nothing about until this point, don't accept any recommendation until you've thoroughly investigated the situation. The school could be looking for candidates for a prefirst classroom. Or teachers may have found your child lacks some skills needed for the first grade. Your child may still be within the normal range, but appears "delayed" when compared with higher-ability or older children.

37

- Be very wary of screening-test results that suggest your child is having difficulties in specific areas, especially if you haven't noticed any. Not only are these tests highly unreliable, but what appears as a problem or even a disability may not be one at all. Never let anyone use the results of a single test to determine whether your child is at risk. The experiences and judgments of parents, caregivers, preschool teachers and kindergarten teachers are critical here. They are as important as the test results.
- If your child has already experienced learning or social difficulties or if you suspect that he will have problems in kindergarten, do some homework before you send him to school. Will the school recommend he be held out or welcome him and help him overcome the difficulties? What services does the school offer to kindergartners, and how will you obtain them? Some schools screen incoming children to determine strengths and weaknesses such as motor control and print knowledge, and then set up programs to help children with weaknesses. Other schools, working under the premise that learning difficulties aren't really detectable until children engage in formal learning, prefer to assist children within the classroom and wait until difficulties emerge that need external assistance. You need to know the school's approach, but keep in mind it may vary from teacher to teacher, too. If this topic doesn't come up in the orientation meetings, then you should raise it if you're concerned. In a large meeting, phrase it generally: "What's your policy and procedures where a child has learning difficulties?" If you prefer not to speak up there, ask one of the presenters privately after the meeting or share your concerns with a teacher or principal later.
- Finally, if your child has been recommended for special services and this comes as a big surprise to you, be sure to read Denny Taylor's book *Learning Denied*. It's about the parents of a kindergartner who challenge a school's diagnosis of their son's so-called learning difficulties. It's not a story with a happy ending, but it's one that any parent of an at-risk child could easily face.

Laurie has had a speech problem since she began to talk, but her pediatrician said she'd outgrow it. She's about to enter kindergarten, and I don't see much improvement. Will the school take care of it?
If Laurie has never received any speech therapy and you're still concerned about it, ask the school about its services. Officials may ask you to meet with the speech therapist before school begins. If your school has a screening process, Laurie's problems will almost certainly be identified, and the school is obligated to provide whatever therapy is needed.

Your pediatrician may well be right: many speech problems take care of themselves. But those that persist need attention. If you're uncomfortable about the school's recommendations, you can always seek a second opinion from a private speech therapist at your own expense.

Colin is very fidgety and doesn't seem to be able to sit still. Should I have him tested for ADD (Attention Deficit Disorder)?
Whether Colin is labeled "ADD" may depend on which specialist you take him to. Too many normally active children are wrongly being labeled "hyperactive" or "ADD." It's a popular diagnosis these days and thousands of children are on central nervous system stimulant drugs because of it. We wonder how many of them truly have attention disorders and how many simply are very active young children. It's possible that Colin is being asked to focus on tasks that are unreasonable for a four- or five-year-old, or he hasn't yet adjusted to the routines, and his inattentiveness may be a direct consequence of these. Try to eliminate other explanations first before assuming Colin has an attention deficit disorder.

Half-day Versus Full-day Kindergarten

There are two basic kinds of kindergartens—full-day and half-day. The full-day program will typically last six hours; half-day, two and three-quarters hours, either in the morning or in the afternoon. Most schools offer either one or the other, but occasionally both will be available in the same school. In these cases, the full-day program is most likely offered to children with special needs.

Some schools' full-day programs meet only on alternate days: the children come to school for a full day three days a week. They get the same amount of time in school as five half days.

There aren't any clear advantages of full days over half days. It really depends on what is done or, in a half-day program, on what the child is doing during the other half of the day. Full-day programs have the edge when they offer a full day's worth of appropriate experiences, especially if what the child would be doing in the other half of the day is inappropriate to their development.

For example, a child is better off in a full-day kindergarten if he or she spends the other half in front of a television. But a full-day program in which children fill in worksheets might be worse than a half day of worksheets and a half day engaged in healthy, outdoor activity or with an active, stimulating caregiver.

What do full-day kindergartens do with the extra time? They include lunch and a rest, plus several "specials" (art, music, physical education, computer). Their approach isn't necessarily different from a half-day program, just longer.

If you have a choice between morning or afternoon kindergarten, consider your child's daily habits. If he's an early riser and still naps in the afternoon, then send him in the morning. If he stays up late at night and likes to sleep in in the morning, give him another year before he has to get up really early. In our experience, a child won't receive better or worse instruction by going to a morning rather than an afternoon class.

Is there any situation where a half-day kindergarten is preferable to a full-day one?
We can think of two. One is when the full-day program is inappropriate for kindergartners, as we've described above. The other is when the child really isn't ready to be away from home for an entire day, either because of separation anxiety or because a full-day program would be too exhausting.

I think a full-day kindergarten would be better because it gets twice as much done. Or does it?
A good half-day kindergarten runs circles around a poorly managed full-day program. More time doesn't necessarily mean better

experiences. Although studies comparing children's performances generally favor the full-day programs over the short run, the long-term benefits aren't at all clear. Some studies have shown that class size, not length of the school day, is what really makes the difference. We think that the quality of the learning outweighs both class size *and* length of day. Look at what goes on in kindergarten rather than measure how much time it lasts.

I'm not sure my child is ready for a full-day program, but he might be later on. I wish I didn't have to decide now.
Some schools start the year with half-day programs and then switch to a full day. It's a great way to ease the transition from home to school, and it allows teachers to get to know the children well before starting a full-day program. Other schools have both half-day and full-day kindergartens, and they should be amenable to having children switch from one to the other if need be. Often, though, you don't have a choice.

Class Size

Kindergarten classes range in size from ten to fifteen at the low end, all the way up to thirty. Eighteen to twenty-four is typical. You can quickly learn your district's policy on class size, the average size of kindergartens in your school, and the actual size of the class your child will be attending (although this figure may fluctuate even after the year begins). Some schools have absolute maximum class sizes—they add classes if the numbers go above the maximum—while others only specify an average.

Class size is more important in kindergarten than in any other grade level. At no time are students so dependent—emotionally, academically, and physically. They aren't used to being with so many other children and so few adults. It takes a while to get used to it. Also, there's a greater range of developmental levels and abilities than in other grades.

A recent large-scale study, carried out over a four-year period in Tennessee, (Mosteller 1995) convincingly shows that children in classes of fifteen to seventeen in kindergarten through grade three do significantly better in reading and math than children in

41

larger classes, even when those larger classes have full-time teachers' aides.

The National Association for the Education of Young Children (NAEYC) recommends a class size of fifteen to eighteen with a single adult, and no more than twenty-five with two adults, one of whom may be a paraprofessional. In light of the Tennessee study results, we agree with the first recommendation but not with the second. We think kindergartens should have no more than eighteen students, with or without an aide. If the your child's class will be in the twenty-six plus range, you need to advocate for smaller class sizes.

In our school, we're debating kindergarten class size. The school says it's willing to hire aides, but still wants to keep classes at around twenty-five. What do you think?

Although many kindergarten teachers might disagree with us, we think small classes are more important than more adults in the classroom, especially if more adults mean larger classes. A full-time aide doesn't necessarily mean students will get twice as much attention.

Schools are hiring four to eight times as many aides as they are teachers, and there's no evidence they improve the quality of learning. That's because aides are rarely trained, even when assigned to assist children with special needs.

We like the aides hierarchy proposed in Allington and Cunningham's book *Schools That Work*. Level 1 aides do clerical work; Level 2 have direct contact with children in noninstructional roles; and Level 3, properly trained, help with instruction. You should be concerned if the aides in your child's kindergarten are helping with instruction but haven't received the proper training.

The kindergartens in our district have on average twenty-eight children, with no aides. What can I do?

First of all, let the school know you think that's far too many. If the kindergartens are half-day, then these numbers are brutal on teachers, too, since they teach two classes. Schools with such classes won't change unless there are parental complaints.

42

Second, get information from NAEYC to back up your argument. They have policy statements on class size and on the use of aides when classes are bigger than eighteen. Raise this issue at PTA meetings and directly with the school board. It won't be easy, and it may take time, but you'll be surprised how effective you can be with good information and persistence.

Multiage Classes

Multiage grouping is a growing trend. In this setup, children of two or more grades are assigned to a teacher or group of teachers. Kindergarten-age children are mixed in with first graders, or more rarely, with first and second graders. In some rural districts, it's the norm because of small enrollments.

There are precedents for mixed groups. Our neighboring state of Vermont still has many one-room schools. Montessori schools have always used multiage grouping for their classes. And most schools in this country were multiage in the nineteenth century.

In Kentucky, all children are now required to be educated with children at least a year older or younger than themselves. However, kindergartners there do not fall under this requirement on a full-time basis, so some of them spend half the day with each other, the other half with first graders. Or they can be combined with first graders, or even with a mixture of first, second, and third graders. Reactions to this new scheme have been mixed. The general consensus seems to be that the younger children benefit most.

The concept has a long history in private schools and does offer some advantages, one of which is that younger children learn a great deal from older children just as they do in large families. And they seem to learn in a much more relaxed and natural way than they do in formal lessons. Also, as we've discovered from colleagues in Montessori schools, children in multiage classrooms are much more cooperative and supportive and much less competitive in their relationships with classmates.

With the right teachers and program, we think kindergartners can thrive in a classroom with preschoolers and first graders and even second graders. But kindergarten is a very special year between home and school, and if children are likely to be lost in

43

the shuffle of a multiage classroom, then we wouldn't support it. And we are adamantly opposed to multiage classrooms that are created simply to solve a problem of uneven numbers in kindergarten and first grade (in other words, for convenience rather than to promote a sound educational practice).

My child is bright and ready to read. Wouldn't he be better off in a multiage classroom that includes first graders?
Not necessarily. If he's placed in anything but a rigid traditional kindergarten, the teacher will nurture his emerging reading abilities and challenge him appropriately. And remember, he's still a five-year-old with a five-year-old's needs, and they differ from those of six- and seven-year-olds. But if you've been told he's too far advanced in all areas of development for kindergarten, a multiage classroom might be a better choice.

Do children do better in a multiage classroom?
We aren't aware of any studies that show such classes are better for academic learning, but there's no question they promote cooperative learning more than single-grade classrooms do. But even this depends on how the teacher structures things. There's often as much variation in children's ages in a single-grade classroom, and good teachers are capable of having children of different ages learn from one another in either setup. One thing we really like is that multiage classrooms break down traditional barriers and expectations between the grades for both teachers and children.

Will my child, who is shy and reserved, be intimidated and afraid to speak up in a multiage classroom?
It's a risk. But in most of the multiage classrooms we know, teachers are very sensitive and they make sure shy children aren't swamped or inhibited by older ones. Again, if the class size is reasonable, this won't be an issue any more than it is in a single-grade classroom.

How can I tell if the multiage classes in my school are for real, or are just a way of solving a numbers problem?

If there's just one multiage classroom, chances are it's solving a numbers problem. But if there are several, that's a good indication that the school is committed to the concept as a genuine alternative to single-grade classrooms. Teachers will tell you whether their multiage classes are for real.

Teacher Experience and Training

What kind of kindergarten teacher should your child have? It's a critical question because the teacher is the single most important factor in almost every classroom in elementary school. That's especially true in the early primary grades, when children are so dependent on adults for their learning.

It's unfortunate, but most states don't think kindergarten teachers need specific training. The prevailing attitude—luckily diminishing—is that anyone can teach this age group because all they do is "play," that kindergarten doesn't really count in a child's education. But most of the kindergarten teachers we know see their job as a serious responsibility. We think the qualities of a teacher at this level are as important as the curriculum. Three qualities stand out.

First, the teacher genuinely needs to care for four-, five-, and six-year-olds and enjoy teaching them. You can easily recognize that kind of teacher: she knows the children well, is happy and upbeat, and obviously likes her profession. She spends time with the children rather than sitting at her desk, gets involved, is on the floor or sitting at those little tables playing, building, reading, and eating with them. She's not afraid to get her hands dirty.

Second, kindergarten teachers need to have solid professional knowledge in child language development, emergent literacy (the beginning stages of reading, writing, speaking, and listening), and children's literature. They should understand appropriate teaching strategies that will ensure that children grow in their literacy, numeracy, and understanding of the world. Such teachers not only have credentials; they attend professional conferences, read and subscribe to professional journals, and are active in professional organizations (e.g., National Association for the Education of Young Children, Association of Childhood Educators International, International Reading Association). If you asked them for advice on what to read about retention, for example, they'd lend you current journal articles or books on the topic or refer you to appropriate titles or sources.

Don't be too quick to judge a teacher's professional knowledge, though, especially in an open house. Some are unusually nervous about addressing parents in this situation and may appear as though they don't know very much. Conversely, there are some teachers with slender professional knowledge who make the slickest presentations!

Third, kindergarten teachers need to be good at communicating with parents. That's especially important in kindergarten because the year isn't just the first school year for the child, it's the first school year for the parent, too. (We discuss this aspect of a teacher's qualities in "Parental Involvement," p. 52).

Will you get a teacher with these qualities? Possibly with all three. More likely with at least two. Occasionally with just one of them. Rarely with none, thank goodness. You have a right to expect highly trained teachers, and schools should be pleased to tell you how well qualified and experienced their teachers are.

I've heard all about Mrs. Ratburn, the kindergarten teacher who yells at children, and I'm scared to death that my child will end up in her classroom. What can I do?

Luckily, teachers like Mrs. Ratburn are pretty rare. Voice your concerns to the principal, but focus on the mismatch between what's best for your child and the approach used in this kindergarten rather than bearing down on Mrs. Ratburn's personal characteristics. While schools are reluctant to admit openly that a teacher isn't up to snuff, they sometimes will transfer one elsewhere if parents persist in their complaints.

How can I tell if the kindergarten teacher my child will have this year is really good or just talks a good game?

Good teachers will have established a strong and positive reputation with colleagues, administrators, and parents. If the reports you get from a wide variety of people are all good, then the teacher's reputation is almost certainly deserved. Signs of talking a good game often involve being a poor listener (you get the feeling the teacher is more interested in his or her own views than in yours), not being very open with parents or to parental suggestions, and not being very knowledgeable about the children or particularly interested in them. Remember, too, that teachers have their strengths and weaknesses. One may communicate poorly with you but be an excellent teacher for your child.

Screening Before Kindergarten

Children face many tests as they proceed through their education, in some cases even before they start school. It's a common practice for incoming kindergartners to be tested for two different purposes. One, sometimes required by state law, is to identify those children at risk for learning difficulties and those with potential talents. The other is to determine children's "developmental" level and make placement recommendations.

Testing is usually done in the spring or summer preceding kindergarten, using formal screening measures such as the Brigance K + 1 Screening or the Dial-R. The Dial-R, for example, tests motor skills (catching, building blocks, copying), concepts (identifying body parts, naming colors, rote counting), and language skills (giving personal data, articulation, remembering). It also indicates social and emotional development.

Developmental screening tests determine placement. They cover tasks found in traditional kindergarten curriculums—writing one's name and address, copying shapes, writing numbers, and so on. The Gesell School Readiness Screening Test is one such widely used test. It rates children as either "ready" or "unready" for kindergarten. If they're "unready," they may be advised not to enter school for another year or be assigned to a prekindergarten program.

Researchers have raised a number of concerns about these screening measures. First, they've been found not to be reliable or valid enough to determine definitely if a child is learning disabled or gifted. If they're used for this purpose without further evaluation of a child's academics and behavior, misdiagnosis is quite likely. If school officials have used only these measures to suggest you place your child in a transitional class or hold him out for another year, challenge them. The tests cannot by themselves provide sufficient information to make such a recommendation.

Second, if children are tested in March and are slated to enter kindergarten in September, their performance may not reflect their capabilities at the time they start school. Over the course of only a few months, they can make remarkable developmental progress. It would be harmful to place a child in a transitional program on the basis of a test whose results are outdated.

A third problem is that if screening indicates a child is not "ready" for kindergarten and he is denied entry, he may not receive the help he would have received in kindergarten. Denying children such services is not just bad educational practice—it may well be illegal in your state.

Recently, many schools have switched to more informal screens, administered in the first week or so of kindergarten by the teachers. Although the timing is different and the instruments themselves may not be the same, remember that their purpose hasn't changed.

One benefit of this kind of small-group screening in the classroom, with children already enrolled, is a more valid assessment of their abilities. The goal of identifying at-risk and potentially gifted children is still attainable, but the results are not used as a final diagnosis. That's the responsibility of the school's support staff (special education, remedial reading, gifted and talented).

Find out what screening measures are administered in your district and the purposes they serve. More important, you need to know the limitations of these measures. Given their poor reliability, be particularly wary of recommendations for holding a child out of kindergarten based solely on test results.

The problem is that most parents (and apparently many educators, too) have no basis on which to question test results, so they assume they must be accurate. The decision to hold a child out of or place a child into kindergarten should always be made on the basis of evidence from a variety of sources—your knowledge and experiences, the kindergarten or preschool teacher's observations, samples of the child's work, and reports from any specialist who's been working with him.

My son David took a placement screening test in March and I was told to hold him out. What should I do?
First, talk with David's preschool teacher (and anyone else who has been involved with David's education so far) and see what she says. Look at the specific items on the test that led to the recommendation, and compare them with what you and others have already observed in David. If this analysis doesn't coincide with the test recommendations, don't hold David out. If there's any doubt, have him screened again in August, when the results may be quite different.

My district doesn't have any screening before kindergarten. How will I know if I should send my child on time?
Don't rely on tests to make your decision. Your own observations of your child, the recommendations of her preschool teacher, and an analysis of the kind of kindergarten she will enter are much more useful and valid sources on which to base your decision.

Testing During Kindergarten

Kindergartners may be given achievement tests late in the year to see how well they are progressing and to help teachers make first-grade placement recommendations. They may also receive "grades" (Satisfactory, Improving, Needs Improvement) for their work in reading, writing, social skills, and so on.

Standardized achievement tests are part of the baggage that came with the academic curriculum when it was forced down into kindergarten in the 1960s, and they aren't appropriate tools for evaluating the progress of very young children. These tests do not generally provide much useful information about kindergartners, and they are particularly unsuited to making recommendations for placement in first grade, if that's what they are used for. So how should a teacher assess a kindergartner's progress, and what should you expect to receive?

Most of what a teacher learns about her students comes from observing them, sampling their work, and talking with them one-on-one or in small groups. Some teachers have checklists to chart each child's progress in reading and writing, math, music, art, and physical education (if done in the classroom). Others prefer to take extended notes and compile these into a narrative that describes a child's strengths and needs.

Teachers have to be alert for signs of persistent difficulties that need a specialist's attention. But teachers are in an excellent position to tell the difference between a child who has genuine difficulties and one whose development is taking a little longer than his peers.

Throughout the year, you should receive information about your child's progress, and not just poor progress. Parent-teacher conferences in the fall and spring are, of course, the formal occasions for sharing this news, but we think informal notes and phone conversations in between conferences are needed, too.

The final communication is the report card. We have examined hundreds of these over the years and worked with teachers trying to improve them. We wish they reflected the major goals of kindergarten better and stated a child's progress in relation to these goals in plain, simple English. Too often, they're jargon-laden lists of behaviors and skills that only other teachers can understand. If one of these tiny skills is marked Needs Improvement, you're likely to worry your child has missed something significant.

We prefer that teachers write narratives about children, and perhaps supplement these with brief checklists that show progress in major areas. We don't think letter or number grades are helpful at this level.

Keep in mind that in the larger scheme of life, a kindergartner's score on a standardized test or a set of letter grades on a report card is not likely to impair her chances of getting into a prestigious college or landing a job interview. What's important is that you fully understand how your child is developing and what, if any, additional help she needs during these formative years.

I'm worried that my child will do poorly on the achievement tests given in kindergarten. Is there anything I should do?
Share your concerns with the kindergarten teacher and see what she does to help children prepare for the test. Resist the temptation to prepare your child yourself—much better to make sure that he or

she gets a good night's sleep and a healthy breakfast on the day of the test. Let your child take the test and see what happens. If the results are fine, that's the end of it. If the results are disappointing and there's no follow-up, let the matter rest. But by all means question a recommendation that your child repeat kindergarten or go into a transitional class if the recommendation is based solely on the test (see also the "Retention" section, p. 29). As long as the results have no immediate consequences, you have little to worry about. Unfortunately, they sometimes do.

Getting your child ready for these tests isn't the issue. Kindergartners shouldn't be taking group standardized tests in the first place. Period. If we could only get school board members, school administrators, and state education officials to observe kindergartners in a group testing situation, they'd never allow it to happen again. They'd see some children calling out the answers, some looking at each other's papers, some becoming so anxious that they get stomachaches or even wet themselves. It's such an unnatural situation for kindergartners. No wonder the test results are so unreliable and invalid!

When my older child Mary was going through kindergarten, I didn't get any feedback from her teacher until nearly the end of the year. How can I be sure this won't happen again with my son Matthew?
In most schools, teachers will give progress reports in writing or in parent conferences at least three times a year. If this doesn't occur, or if you feel your concerns are not being addressed, then contact the teacher and request a conference.

Tamara got an Unsatisfactory in something called "Auditory Discrimination" on her kindergarten report card. What is this, and what should I be doing about it?
It's the child's ability to detect differences in spoken sounds. The fact that Tamara got an Unsatisfactory isn't that important, and there's really no need to worry at this stage, especially if generally she's been doing well in kindergarten. Most likely, she'll learn to read perfectly well without any additional instruction in this skill.

51

In fact, her auditory discrimination will probably improve as her reading progresses. We don't think specific skills like these ought to be on report cards. They only make parents like you think there's something wrong, and they often lead to inappropriate practices like sending children off to a tutorial center.

Parental Involvement

Polly Greenberg, writing in the journal *Young Children,* reminds us that public schools were originally founded and run by parents. How things have changed! As schools have become more professionalized and bureaucratic, parents have increasingly been squeezed out of meaningful roles, making many feel alienated and powerless.

Parent involvement is a tricky issue. To what extent should schools involve you in designing and implementing programs? Should you be treated as clients or customers and given what you want? Or is your proper responsibility to support and carry out the school's programs?

Recently, parental involvement has become a key item in educational reform. For the first time in years, parents have been participating in the governance of public schools at all levels, including setting goals and designing curriculum. In some schools, parental representatives are carefully screened and there are so few of them that their influence may be marginal. In others, parents are full partners with teachers and administrators and have enormous influence.

There are several aspects of this that are worth thinking about. The first is choice. How much choice should you have in a public school? Should schools offer you a variety of kindergarten programs and let you choose the one you want? If you want a particular approach to kindergarten, should the school provide it? Should you be allowed to choose your child's teacher?

We think schools should offer parents as much choice as they can. This is easier to do if all the kindergarten classes are in one building and if there are many of them. It's harder in small school districts or in large districts with widely scattered schools. But there's a downside to choice. More options mean more busing, and that breaks up neighborhood schools.

If enough parents are advocating for kindergarten programs the school doesn't currently offer, they need to be accommodated. We are less sympathetic to individual parents advocating for programs that are at one extreme or the other (a program in which children are free to do whatever they like all day long, say, or a program based on strict Christian fundamentalist principles) or for a highly specific approach (e.g., a program that only teaches phonics, or does so with a specified commercial program). Public schools have to adhere strictly to the principle of separation of church and state, and they are not likely to offer programs that lean philosophically too far to the left or to the right. Parents seeking these kinds of programs are better served in the private sector, or through home-schooling.

But you should make your views known to the school, especially if you feel available programs don't reflect, even in small measure, what you want for your child's first school experience. Changes may not come as quickly as you'd like, but at least when the opportunity arises to hire a new kindergarten teacher, the issue will be raised. And as more parents become part of the committees that hire new teachers, their voices are much more likely to be heard.

Of course, you can't choose between alternatives you know nothing about, so the school needs to present, in its brochures and orientation meetings, a clear description of existing alternatives. You should also have the opportunity to see the different programs in action (see page 66 for our advice on how to do this).

Should you pick your child's teacher? This is one of the worst-kept secrets in the business. People routinely do, even though most schools have policies that strictly forbid it. We have mixed feelings here. On the one hand, we don't think teachers should be put up to bid, even though this would quickly weed out those with poor reputations. On the other hand, making a good match between parents, their children, and a classroom can't be a bad thing. We think a school can be sensitive to a parent's request for a teacher or program without necessarily launching a bidding war.

If you want your child to have a particular teacher, you're better off requesting the kind of program the teacher offers rather than a certain person (see below). Program requests are more likely to be honored than those for individuals—personalities are more easily kept out of it.

How teachers and parents interact with one another during the child's kindergarten year is also a critical aspect of parental involvement.

- You should be welcomed as a volunteer in the classroom if you're willing and available. You should work under the teacher's guidance and not try to take over the class, however. Even if you can't volunteer, you should be invited to participate in other ways (perhaps making things and bringing them in).
- Two-way communication between teachers and parents is critical. Successes as well as concerns should be conveyed in a timely way. You should feel comfortable telling teachers about events and circumstances that relate to your child's well-being.
- Teachers must be approachable. You should be able to express your feelings without fear of being embarrassed or criticized. And you should expect conversations to be confidential.
- Teachers need to respect your views, experiences, and background, to truly listen to your concerns, and to avoid patronizing you. Sensitivity to different religious and cultural beliefs is a hallmark of a respectful teacher. But they should not shy away from saying things that need to be said (even unpleasant truths can be related in a tactful and respectful manner).
- Teachers need to communicate with all parents, not just the supportive ones; they also need to adapt to parents' schedules.

If your experience falls somewhat short of these ideals, don't take it personally. As Polly Greenberg points out, teachers aren't usually trained to work with the many kinds of parents they're likely to encounter. In fact, parent involvement is a topic that rarely even surfaces in their training. Of particular concern is a teacher's ability to work with parents from backgrounds and with experiences that are very different from her own. If your teacher isn't a great communicator, take heart. She may still be very good with your child, and that's the most important thing.

And teachers are human, too. They make mistakes. Sometimes they're so busy they neglect something that's important to you or your child. While it's appropriate to remind a teacher of her obligations to keep in touch with you, it doesn't hurt occasionally to tell her just how well she's doing or how much your child enjoyed a particular activity. Teaching is a very stressful occupation, and among all the daily difficulties, it's very refreshing to get a nice note from a parent.

I've heard that there's only one developmentally appropriate kindergarten program in the school my child is going to. How can I be sure my child will get into this class?
You stand a much better chance of choosing a particular program than you do a particular teacher. Ask that your child be placed in a developmentally appropriate program and give your reasons. The better you are able to articulate the kind of program you think your child will thrive in, the more likely your request will be granted.

I want to volunteer in my child's kindergarten but the teacher doesn't allow parents of currently enrolled children to volunteer. What gives?
This is common, and it's sad to see teachers missing out on a great opportunity to involve parents in their classrooms. But it's their choice. Raise the issue with the teachers, the principal, and the parent-teacher group. Find out why your child's teacher feels as she does and try to allay her fears. Bonnie couldn't imagine her kindergarten without the children's parents as volunteers—it's a critical component of her approach.

I've volunteered in my child's kindergarten, but my daughter clings to me all day and the teacher has suggested I don't volunteer. Any ideas?
Explain to your daughter that while you're in the classroom, she needs to be with the other children and not with you. Tell her that

you are in the classroom to help all the children, not just her. Try volunteering in other ways for now and come back to the class later, when she may be less clingy.

I work at a full-time job, so I can't volunteer in the classroom. Is there anything else I can do?
It's frustrating to both you and your child that you can't be there like other parents. But maybe you can come in for short periods, or volunteer in other ways, like helping out with after-school projects or making things to bring in. Also, you might want to ask a spouse or a family member to stand in for you so that your child doesn't feel that he or she is the only child whose parent doesn't participate. Teachers can help, too, by not inadvertently criticizing parents whose schedules or jobs prevent them from volunteering.

It really bothers me that the kindergarten my child is enrolled in celebrates Halloween. Halloween has no place in my religious beliefs. What can I do?
Express your concerns to the teacher and see how you and your child's religious beliefs can be accommodated. Halloween is such a firmly entrenched part of the kindergarten experience in many schools that it's not likely to be abandoned to suit an individual parent. Maybe your child can be excused from the celebrations. On the other hand, if a number of parents express their concern about using instructional time for Halloween parades and parties, the school might reconsider its practices. You may be surprised to find that many teachers agree with you on this issue and would be happy to get parental support.

Other Issues

Because we work with young children and their parents every day, we're often asked about our views. Here are some of the most commonly asked questions having to do with issues we haven't covered specifically earlier in this chapter.

I worry that if my child goes to a whole language or developmentally appropriate kindergarten, and then into a traditional first grade, she'll find the transition too difficult. Should I place her in a traditional kindergarten to be on the safe side?

Children are much more resilient and adaptable than we give them credit for, and it's unlikely that the switch from a whole language or developmentally appropriate kindergarten to a traditional first grade will be all that traumatic. Look at it this way: at least your daughter will have had the benefits of a kindergarten you think is appropriate for her. That's better than having two years of what you think is inappropriate. And you may find that your school also has first- and second-grade classrooms that teach with a whole language or developmentally appropriate approach, so there won't be a transitional problem.

I have twins. Our school has two kindergartens, each with different philosophies. Should I ask that they be placed in the same class or in different ones?

If one program is clearly superior to the other, then try to put them both in it. Most likely the teacher will give the twins the autonomy they need. If you're concerned that they won't be sufficiently separated during the school day, then keep them apart for activities outside of school. If the two programs differ in philosophy but are both excellent, then you might want to consider one twin in each. In any event, be sure to sit down and share your concerns with the teachers or the principal.

My child has severe allergic reactions to bee stings. What should I do to alert the kindergarten teacher?

Alert the school nurse to your child's allergy first. But make sure the teacher knows about it, because you can't assume the nurse will have relayed the information, especially at the very beginning of the school year. Ask the teacher to tell the other teachers and playground personnel, and make sure there's a system for automatically alerting substitutes, too. Your child must also take responsibility for alerting people to the allergy and knowing what to do, since those who are aware might not be around when she gets stung.

I'm divorced, and my ex-husband isn't allowed, by court order, to have any contact with my son. How can I be sure that he won't

come to school and take him away?
Schools are getting more security conscious these days and generally don't allow visitors without proper authorization. But it isn't difficult for a determined adult to gain access to a child in the playground or in the confusion of dismissal. Let the principal and the kindergarten teacher know the specifics of the court order, preferably in writing, and what procedures should be followed if your ex-husband shows up at the school. Good communication between you and the school is essential, but teachers are not security guards and can only go so far to protect a child from unwarranted contact by family members.

I'm divorced, and my daughter lives with her mother. But I have visiting rights, and I want to be fully involved in Linda's kindergarten. What should I do?
Make sure the teacher knows about your situation. Depending on what you and your ex-wife work out, you can attend all school functions together, alternate them, or ask for separate parent-teacher conferences (most teachers we know will do this for parents). A good idea is to make up some self-addressed envelopes and ask the teacher to send you anything that's normally sent out to parents. If you volunteer, do it on different days from your ex-wife.

Teachers try to accommodate the special needs of divorced parents, but make sure you keep your family disputes out of the classroom, if you volunteer, and out of teacher meetings, unless they're relevant to a current situation.

I've heard that my child's kindergarten class will have two or three special education students "mainstreamed" this year. I worry that my child will suffer if all the attention is given to these students.
Children with special needs have a right to be educated in the least restrictive environment, and their placement in regular classes is their right by law. Bonnie's experience has been very positive—her kindergartners have learned a lot from children with disabilities. But if a child's needs are so severe that the classroom is constantly disrupted, then something has to be done so everyone can learn.

Full-time aides are usually available in those cases, so a disabled child will rarely have to be placed in an alternative setting.

But if disruptions in your child's class are interfering with learning, raise the issue and expect that something will be done about it. Our experience is that for every situation in which special-needs children are allowed to learn with their peers that doesn't work out, there are ten that immeasurably enrich the special-needs students' sense of inclusion and social development and the other students' understanding.

I'm worried that my son Jarrett and my next-door neighbor's child, who really don't get along, are going to be in the same kindergarten. Should I just grin and bear it?
Tell the principal. It may be that without hurting either child's possibilities for a good year, they can be placed in different classrooms. Or, you might be assured that if it doesn't work out, the assignments can be changed after a month or so. At least the school will be alerted to the situation.

Our family's primary language is Spanish, and my daughter's barely able to speak English. Is this going to be a problem in kindergarten?
We must admit we have little experience with ESL (English as a Second Language) children. We don't have personal knowledge of kindergartens taught entirely in Spanish, for example. But all the ESL children Bonnie has taught over the years have picked up sufficient English during kindergarten (more easily, obviously, where at least some English is spoken at home; much more slowly if it isn't) to be able to go on to first grade.

It's surprising how quickly children learn a language they're immersed in every day, particularly when they're actively encouraged to talk and share what they know. But you may need to seek help from the school's bilingual staff or elsewhere if your child doesn't seem to be learning reasonably quickly, especially if there is no English spoken at home.

We'd like to end this chapter with a story, set in suburbia, that shows the pressures operating on parents to conform to neighborhood expectations. It takes quite a bit of determination and persistence to withstand them.

Leslie and Abigail's story

Leslie and Abigail are the daughters of Mark and Judy Hazelton. Just before enrolling Leslie in kindergarten, the Hazeltons moved into a new housing development. The majority of the residents were well educated, professional people. Within a few days, Judy's neighbors informed her that Leslie would be going into a "whole language" kindergarten and she should contact the principal immediately and have her transferred to the "regular" kindergarten in the same building.

As Judy tells it: "I'd never heard about whole language. But my instinct was to find out about it, and as I did, it sounded very interesting to me, and very similar to the kind of preschool program Leslie had attended. So I didn't ask for her to be changed. But I did have some doubts as to whether this was the right idea. So I approached the kindergarten teacher and said, 'This is what my neighbors are telling me about your program.' She explained her approach, and it seemed very sensible to me. But I was still nervous. We could afford a private school, and I asked the teacher about a prestigious private school in the area. The teacher knew it by reputation, but hadn't visited, so we went together. It wasn't any different from Leslie's kindergarten, only $5,000 more expensive! So Leslie went to public school and had a great year, and she's done well ever since."

Abigail, their younger daughter, had had some medical problems as a toddler that left her at risk for a learning disability or attention deficit disorder. Her birthday was August 26, and Judy was more than a little nervous about sending her to kindergarten the first year she was eligible, especially when neighbors were holding back children with May birthdays! She talked with the kindergarten teacher, who told her that differences between children generally even out by third grade and that she should send her to school on time. Was there a better placement for Abigail? Judy couldn't think of one.

Over the summer, Judy hired a tutor to work with Abigail on her numbers, letters, and writing for three hours a week. "Part of the reason I wanted Abigail to go to kindergarten on time is that there were four other girls of her age in our neighborhood and I didn't want her to have the stigma of going to school later than they did. I didn't like the pressure, but it was there." So Judy sent Abigail to kindergarten, where she held her head slightly above water, with tutoring twice a week. Judy's anxieties surfaced again by January. Should Abigail be retained in kindergarten? By April, she upped the tutoring to three days a week so that Abigail's achievement tests would show good results. As luck would have it, Abigail wasn't feeling well on the day of the tests and did very poorly. Judy and the teacher decided that Abigail should go on, despite these results, since she'd be assigned to a particularly good first-grade teacher, also with a whole language philosophy.

Abigail started first grade a little shakily but by January, she had blossomed. She's now in third grade, and doing fine.

What we'd like you to remember from this story is that Judy stuck to her guns, but not without doubts or without the "insurance" of a tutor for Abigail. What we especially admire is that she did her homework so that she could make up her own mind about which program she wanted for her children and when she wanted them to begin it.

Chapter Three

Doing Your Homework

Joshua

If this were the sixties and you were sending your child to kindergarten, there wouldn't be alternatives to choose from. You would attend an orientation, perhaps have a meeting with the teacher, and in some places, maybe even receive a home visit from the teacher before your child started school. Almost certainly, the kindergarten would be a traditional readiness program. The idea that public schools should treat parents as clients had not yet arrived, so it would be unthinkable for you to raise questions (as opposed to simply asking them) about the kind of kindergarten your child would be entering.

But times have changed. Not only are there different approaches to kindergarten, which we describe in Chapter 1, but schools more frequently see parents as partners in their children's education these days. Teachers and administrators increasingly listen to parents' views, even if they don't always act on them. Also, many parents are no longer willing simply to accept on faith what educators tell them—they want to know more about kindergarten for themselves.

We'd like you to become better informed about your school's kindergarten philosophy and practice. We believe the more you know, the better equipped you'll be to choose what's appropriate for your child and the less anxious you'll be about the process.

So how do you find out what's going on? And what information do you need?

Examining What the School Sends You Ahead of Time

What is the district saying about its kindergarten philosophy and programs? Most schools provide written descriptions of all grade-level programs, although we've found that many of them are vague, full of platitudes and educational jargon.

You should at least be able to locate a written curriculum, even though it may have been designed for teachers rather than parents. But be careful! There's no guarantee that it accurately describes what goes on in the classroom. Such documents are usually created by committees every five to ten years, circulated among the faculty, and then often filed away. They may reflect current practices when they're written, but they are updated infrequently at best. They may also minimize differences in philosophy and practice among teachers or schools in the district or pretend that those differences don't exist.

Even so, what the district publishes for teachers and parents is revealing. For example, a brochure that clearly lays out a school's early childhood education philosophy, goals, and kindergarten programs, tells you the district has thought about these issues and is committed to sharing its views with parents. On the other hand, a district that publishes nothing sends a clear message about what it thinks parents ought to know.

Brochures like this should ideally include the following elements, although it's unlikely that the brochure you receive will cover all of them:

- The underlying philosophy guiding the school's approach to kindergarten.
- The relationship of kindergarten to first grade, prefirst/ transition (if any), and the rest of the elementary school.
- The goals of kindergarten. What does the program strive for? Is it readiness for first grade? Growth in specific areas? A period of self-initiated play before a child starts academics in earnest in first grade?
- A brief description of the curriculum. What kinds of things will kindergartners be doing? What will be

"covered"? How is the program organized? Are there different approaches in place?

- Expectations for incoming kindergartners. Are there criteria established for children's "readiness"? Are there skills they should have already mastered? Are there circumstances under which a child will be recommended not to enroll in kindergarten on schedule?
- Screening and testing before children start kindergarten and during the year. What screening and/or testing procedures are used? For what purposes? How are the results used? Communicated to parents?
- Retention policy and procedures. Under what circumstances will children be retained? Sent to prefirst or transitional class? How many children are retained, and why?
- Listing of faculty, including their qualifications, experience, and a short paragraph of introduction.
- Kindergarten requirements (listing of policies and procedures for clothing, supplies, parental involvement, report cards, parent-teacher conferences, and the like).

It doesn't matter if this information comes from the district in a single brochure, as handouts from an individual school, in notes from the teacher, or in some combination of these. What matters is that you have what you need before your child starts kindergarten.

Attending Your School's Kindergarten Orientation

Almost all schools hold an orientation session for the parents of incoming kindergartners, usually in the spring. Go and take notes. Pay attention to what the presenters say about the purpose of their kindergarten, the curriculum, their expectations for entering children, the criteria for promotion to first grade, and testing procedures and instruments (if any).

The session should reveal something about the philosophy and program. If you hear about prerequisite skills (following directions, knowing letters and sounds, counting to ten, sitting still) that kindergartners need so they'll be ready for first grade, you can be pretty sure the school has a traditional approach. This will be confirmed if school officials tell you children will be retained in kindergarten for an additional year (or placed in a prefirst or transitional class) if they don't meet first-grade expectations.

If the officials refer to their program as developmentally appropriate, how do they define this term? If they spell out most or all of the principles we list on page 6 (fitting the kindergarten curriculum to the child, taking children as far as they can go, emphasizing growth not mastery, accepting children into first grade at the level they've achieved), then they're at least espousing a developmentally appropriate philosophy. If they refer to the National Association for the Education of Young Children's (NAEYC) guidelines, that's another good sign. But since *developmentally appropriate* is a popular new term, some educators will adopt it even though they don't subscribe to its philosophy or fully understand it.

Do they perhaps define developmentally appropriate in terms of a traditional program "appropriate" for a child's "development," as "waiting" until a child is mature enough to be taught reading and writing, or as giving a child "the gift of time"? Then they mean something quite different. Note any inconsistencies: if officials claim their program is developmentally appropriate but talk about entry requirements for both kindergarten and first grade, you know something isn't right.

Officials may also describe their philosophy as *whole language*. You know that approach is indeed in place if they say that learning to read and write is as natural as learning to speak, that the curriculum should be child-centered, that the teacher should facilitate children's learning rather than direct it, that children should be immersed in print. They may refer to the work of Ken and Yetta Goodman or quote from Bobbi Fisher's book *Joyful Learning*. Unfortunately, the term *whole language* is used very loosely in schools; unless it's used in conjunction with a clear explanation of how the approach is carried out, you won't know if the school or its teachers are really committed to it.

If brochures or presentations still confuse you, don't be too alarmed. Although all public schools have kindergartens, not all of them have a philosophy or are able to articulate it. In many schools, kindergarten is simply kindergarten, and all parents are told is what their children should bring to school, what the school policies are, how much lunch costs, and so on.

There will be no misunderstanding at a Waldorf or Montessori orientation. These schools can't call themselves Waldorf or Montessori if they didn't subscribe to and practice a certain philosophy. Waldorf schools espouse one basic philosophy, as we discuss in Chapter 1. The philosophy of Montessori schools differs slightly depending on whether they adhere to the traditional approach or advocate a "reformed" Montessori philosophy. (Again, see Chapter 1 for a detailed discussion.)

We wish public schools were as consistent as Montessori and Waldorf schools are in getting their philosophy across. It's more than a communication problem. A public school may have a great philosophy it can't articulate or doesn't follow, or it may have several philosophies, or none. You can't assume from brochures or orientation meetings that the school practices what it preaches. You may need to dig a little deeper.

Talking to Other Parents About Their Experiences

Talk to parents of children who've been through kindergarten in your district. They won't be shy about sharing their views of teachers and programs. But ask them to describe, not judge. Ask about what went on in class, what the teacher was trying to accomplish, how different aspects of the curriculum were treated, and so on.

For example, learning from a parent that a program you heard described as developmentally appropriate at the orientation consisted mainly of ditto sheets on the letters of the alphabet shows you there's no genuine understanding or commitment to that approach. But it's a relief to hear that a teacher who has a reputation for being somewhat harsh with children is regarded as quite the opposite by the parent of a child who was in her program last year.

And remember that every kindergarten teacher is liked by some parents and not liked by others. So don't use fellow parents as a sole source for learning about what goes on in kindergarten.

Observing a Kindergarten Class in Your School

While we don't think parents should be invited (nor ask to be invited) into kindergarten classrooms en masse—that would seriously interfere with the program—we do think you should be welcomed individually. So our advice is, if you don't feel you received enough information in brochures and orientation sessions, or if you're seriously considering alternatives, ask to spend time in the classrooms to see firsthand what actually happens there. But it may be hard to gain access. Many schools discourage visitors in their classrooms, either because they feel it's disruptive or because they don't want prospective parents scouting out the options, so you have to be sensitive to that.

If possible, visit several programs. All teachers rarely have the same philosophy or approach, so a visit to one classroom might be very misleading. Spending time in the one developmentally appropriate kindergarten may leave you with the impression that all the kindergartens in the school take this approach. Conversely, you may think all classes are like the traditional one you visited.

Remember too that what a teacher does in front of visitors may not represent a typical day. To get a true picture, you would have to visit each classroom more than once, and that's not practical. So even if you do manage to spend time in a classroom or two, be careful about the conclusions you draw. Balance your observations with other information.

A school that's confident about its kindergarten philosophy and practices will grant your request to visit classrooms. You'll more likely be refused in schools that lack a philosophy or are suspicious of parents "poking around" or if you are obnoxious and come into the school with an "agenda" or a closed mind.

Be prepared for the argument, "We can't allow you to visit a kindergarten because if we did, we'd have hundreds of such requests." If you immediately get your back up, administrators and teachers will get defensive. Emphasize that you aren't looking for the best teacher for your child (that's what will be assumed, no matter what you say) but rather for information about the program. You and your child are, after all, the school's clients.

If you do arrange a visit, make it productive. First, talk with the teacher ahead of time so you arrive at a mutually convenient time. Ask about how the teacher would like you to interact with her and the students. Some like visitors to mingle with the children and participate in the classroom as an extra adult, while others would rather you stay out of the way and be as invisible as possible. Few teachers like to be interrupted, so don't interrupt a lesson with questions unless you're specifically invited to. Talk afterward with the teacher about what went on and about variations in other classrooms. Teachers, more than anyone, know what's really going on, and they'll be much more willing to share what they know one-on-one than they are in an orientation meeting. But remember they have very little free time during the day, so keep this meeting as brief as you can.

Instead of judging the program, ask the teacher to clarify or explain aspects of it. Teachers who feel threatened or defensive by your visit or who feel you're imposing your views on them will clam up. This sort of attitude may also mark you as a trouble-maker. While your child probably won't suffer as a consequence, you'll acquire an aura of suspicion that will quickly circulate around the faculty and administration and may persist through the kindergarten year and possibly further.

Just watch, listen, and learn without expressing your own point of view or debating teachers or administrators. If your visit is perceived as simply an opportunity to confirm negative opinions, you would have been better off staying home. You may indeed form a negative impression from the visit, but it's not a smart strat- egy to share that impression while you're there.

No one will label you a troublemaker if you spend your visit time observing, asking questions, and being polite. Acting inno- cent is one of the best ways to learn. Coming in with an attitude is guaranteed to produce little learning and a lot of hostility, neither of which is really what you need.

You'll not have any of these kinds of problems if you decide to visit a private school's kindergarten. Private schools will go out of their way to show you around, let you sit in on classes, and attend to all your questions and concerns. And it makes sense, if you're at all worried about whether you're making the right choice, to check out all the options in your area. You may even find that a private school that you assumed was beyond your means had scholarships available.

Learning More About Kindergarten

Because you're reading this book, you already want to know more about kindergarten, and what you're reading here may be sufficient for your present needs. After all, when you visit the doctor or dentist, how much do you really need to know about medicine or dentistry?

On the other hand, we wrote this book so you could become better informed about kindergarten, so we wouldn't be at all surprised if you wanted to learn more and we'd be delighted to know we prompted you to dig in.

For example, if your child has been recommended for retention and you're adamantly opposed to it, you may have to prepare your case quite thoroughly, especially if the school is applying pressure. In her book *Learning Denied*, Denny Taylor describes how a child, Patrick, and his parents were put through the wringer over a three-year period because of Patrick's so-called learning problems in kindergarten. Although the parents were ultimately unsuccessful in rebuffing the school's faulty diagnosis of Patrick's difficulties—they ended up taking Patrick out of school and educating him at home—they read extensively about testing, learning disabilities, and related topics like state law. We wonder whether the outcome wouldn't have been more successful if Patrick's parents had been better informed much earlier on.

If you want to learn more about any of the issues we discuss in Chapter 2, start with the books and articles listed in the Endnotes. If you read them, you'll become very knowledgeable.

But there are other ways to deepen and extend your knowledge of early childhood education:

- Keep an eye out for guest lectures at local colleges and universities.
- Browse through some of the early childhood journals and magazines in your local public library. Journals like *Young Children* and *Childhood Education* are aimed at educators, but occasionally there'll be an article about parental involvement or some other issue you're very interested in. Popular magazines such as *Parenting* or *Redbook* do sometimes have articles about kindergarten, and they're usually readable and informative.
- Take courses or workshops at your local school, teacher center, community college, or university. Sometimes it's

more pleasant to learn in the company of others because of what you gain from fellow students.

- Organize a study group in cooperation with your parent-teacher association, the kindergarten teachers, or fellow parents. Choose one topic at a time, and then read about it and discuss it in the group. This approach is much less threatening than taking a course, but has many of the same benefits.
- Join a professional organization like the National Association for the Education of Young Children (NAEYC). It welcomes parents as well as educators, and its conferences and publications are aimed at both groups.
- Do your own reading on these issues. Follow through on some of our suggestions for further reading, or browse through the education section in a public library or bookstore. Ask kindergarten teachers, public and school librarians, and salespeople in bookstores for their recommendations.

Will you be a less effective parent if you do none of these? Should you feel guilty if you haven't started a study group? Of course not. Both you and your child can have an excellent kindergarten experience without your becoming an expert or even delving too deeply into the philosophy and practice of early childhood education.

However, if problems arise, you may need to research your options and become better prepared to refute an "expert" course of action you feel isn't the right one for your child.

Chapter Four

Preparing Your Child for Kindergarten

Are you worried about what you should or shouldn't be doing with your four-year-old before kindergarten starts? Relax. You're probably doing everything just fine.

The transition from home to school can be scary for parents and for children both. But it's been eased somewhat because most children have had some experience with preschool programs. Many of them know what it's like to be separated from their parents for several hours a day.

But there's still something special about kindergarten because it's the beginning of formal schooling. The building itself is probably larger than your child's preschool, and to a person less than four feet tall, it can seem very daunting indeed. And there are so many other children—more and bigger than the familiar faces at home or in preschool. (For a fascinating account of a child's first encounter with school as re-created by a primary school principal, see Liz Waterland's *The Bridge to School*.)

Children usually settle in quickly. But knowing that everything will work out fine doesn't necessarily allay the concerns—even fears—you both may have. There are many things you can do to get your child ready. Some are specifically designed to help ease the transition into a school environment, and a few are geared toward a particular kindergarten approach. We do not believe children should be hurried in their development or forced to do things they aren't ready for. But it's foolish not to take advantage of the many opportunities that present themselves to nurture your child's intellectual, social, aesthetic, and physical development.

Intellectual Development

By intellectual development, we mean a child's emerging literacy, numeracy, and cognitive abilities, including:

- Speaking and listening, already fairly well advanced by the age of four.
- Reading and writing, barely begun at this age.
- Mathematical processing, also barely begun.
- Knowledge of the world—science, animals, people, and so on, which is probably more advanced than we give children credit for.

Let's talk a little about each of these, and how you might nurture your child's growth in these areas.

Speaking and Listening

Four-year-olds are better talkers than listeners, especially when we want them to do something they don't want to do! The best way to nurture their speaking and listening abilities is to talk about everyday topics. Each time you explain something to your child or he or she tells you about something that happened or asks a question or you rephrase something your child has said, you are affirming the importance of language.

Children need to see adults as interesting sources of information, not just direction givers. How much you talk isn't nearly as important as what you say. If all your child hears from you revolves around behavior, then he sees language as merely the means for controlling behavior. But if he hears all sorts of interesting things about the world, he'll learn that adults have worthwhile things to say. What starts as listening to interesting parents is soon followed by listening to interesting teachers.

To promote your child's speaking and listening abilities, share your knowledge, tell about things you're interested in, what fascinates you. Ask him to share what he knows. Why did he choose this toy? What does he like about it? What is he doing with it? What is he pretending it is?

When you answer a child's questions, you enlarge his knowledge of the world and encourage him to ask about new things. When you ask what he's doing, you can model "correct" language in a way that doesn't interfere with the conversation or inhibit him from trying out new forms of language. Repeating what a child has said in a correct form, if not overdone, is a particularly good way of achieving this. But correcting language or communicating displeasure with approximations of adult language doesn't help. Children have to see language as a useful tool, not as something on which they are judged.

Preschoolers need adult guidance to develop language. It doesn't happen on its own. Follow your child's lead. Don't underestimate the importance of talk at this crucial stage of development. As Joan Tough puts it:

> Our plea is that talking should be recognized as providing, for young children at least, the major route to learning. And when we say learning, we are not referring to the learning of language itself but to learning generally. It is the child's capacity for talking that should be used for extending his thinking, for developing ways of using language that will serve him well, and that will provide him with strategies for learning.

Reading

Preschoolers aren't ready to be taught reading (or writing) in the traditional sense, but it isn't too early to be laying the foundations. *The most important thing is to read to your child daily, making it as pleasurable and as comfortable as you can.* Research has proven that children who were read to regularly before they went to school find reading easier to learn and become stronger readers.

Read in bed, in a favorite chair, in a bean bag on the floor next to where you keep your books. Read the old favorites your mother and father read to you as well as new contemporary stories —and read them again and again. Let your child select books too; take her with you to the library regularly. If your library allows it, get her her own card.

If you're stumped for suitable books for four-year-olds, it's easy to get help. Public librarians are great sources, and they have the books at hand for you to borrow. Bookstores are good too. Friends and neighbors can tell you which books their children enjoyed, and often still have copies they might lend you. Garage sales are gold mines for books at bargain prices. And books make great birthday and holiday gifts.

There are many useful guides on selecting titles, such as Jim Trelease's *The Read-Aloud Handbook,* Nancy Larrick's *A Parent's Guide to Children's Reading,* and Eden Lipson's *New York Times Parent's Guide to the Best Books for Children.* In the last fifteen years there has been an explosion of children's books, particularly nonfiction. You can find books on just about any topic suitable for preschoolers. Some deal specifically with children going to school for the first time, and they might be good choices for read-alouds as "the day" gets closer. They include E. Bram's *I Don't Want to Go to School,* R. Caudill's *A Pocketful of Cricket,* Miriam Cohen's *Will I Have a Friend?,* J. Hamilton-Merritt's *My First Days of School,* James Howe's *When You Go to Kindergarten,* Ellen Senisi's *Kindergarten Kids,* and R. Wells's *Timothy Goes to School.*

Children need to see you reading in a variety of settings to begin valuing it. Read the newspaper, magazines, the mail, recipes, coupons, shopping lists, and family messages, and share what you are reading with your child. If Aunt Kim sends you a card telling you about her new job in Nebraska, read parts of it aloud. Show your child the print as you read it, so he or she starts to see the connection between print and meaning. By doing this, you're communicating that reading is important in your life and it eventually will be in his, too. Through these little encounters with text in natural settings, you are beginning to include the child in what Frank Smith calls the "Literacy Club."

Preschoolers can start learning the "code" of reading informally, but don't think of this as something they need for kindergarten. Some are simply not ready to take even these small steps toward becoming actual readers until well into first grade. A few precocious ones start reading at age three, but most begin sometime between five and seven.

How will you know if your child is ready to start? You'll notice he begins to recognize letters in his name and on familiar signs (the *D*'s in Dunkin' Donuts). He shows more than a passing interest in print, tries to identify letters and words on cereal boxes, reads signs while riding in the car, and shows special interest in the actual words of a story you're reading.

Our daughter Katharine, at age two, recognized the K in Kmart, and commented, "Oh! That's a *K* for Katharine!" At age four, while in preschool, our son Jonathan displayed little interest in letter recognition, even though he loved to be read to (he reads fine, now, in eighth grade). Interest in the code may happen overnight, or it may come quite gradually. It may not come until the child is in kindergarten or first grade.

Once a child shows interest in letters, words, and print in general, follow her lead. Books, a set of magnetic letters on the refrigerator, an alphabet puzzle, and simple games are all you need.

The best way to learn the code is in the context of the reading you have already been doing. For example, when you read a rhyming book, let your son or daughter fill in the rhyming words. Select books that are predictable or that have a pattern. After a few hearings, the child will want to "read" along with you. Later, you might want to select very easy books and let the child pick out simple words (*the, I, to*). Later still, you might even let your child create sentences from words cut out of cardboard and have him or her read these.

You'll know when you've gone too far, because any child loses interest in an activity that doesn't give pleasure or satisfaction. Friction between the two of you is another sign that you're overdoing it. If either of these things happens, stop reading and do something else. If you persist, you'll run the real risk of turning the child off to reading.

It's better to avoid "teaching" reading than to harm a child's disposition toward it. Kindergarten teachers don't expect children to be able to decode the words on a printed page, and a child who has been force-fed early will not necessarily become a better reader later on. Butler and Clay's book *Reading Begins at Home* offers some good advice: even if your child becomes fascinated with learning to read, don't stop reading to her! Another excellent book, David Doake's *Reading Begins at Birth*, has many practical suggestions too.

We took an informal survey of kindergarten teachers from different parts of the country to see what academic and social skills they expected of children entering their classes. None anticipated that children would be able to recognize letters or read words or sentences, but they told us they wish parents would read to their children every day.

Writing

In some respects, reading and writing are different sides of the same coin. Both involve meaning, letters, and words, but in reading, you are figuring out what someone else has written. In writing, you're creating text for others to read.

There are two aspects to writing: composing, which entails communicating something to someone else (a thank you letter, a story, a description of an event); and transcribing, which is the business of getting the words down on the page. Transcribing involves spelling, handwriting, and written conventions such as punctuation and capitalization. Preschoolers aren't that good at transcribing. But they have stories to tell, and they can, under the right circumstances, "write."

Children can begin to learn to write quite naturally. *Provide your child with a place and materials for writing, and let him experiment.* A writing place could be as simple as a small table in the family room or kitchen. Materials should include a box or can full of regular pencils, colored pencils, markers, and pens; and paper, preferably without lines. Computer paper or the back sides of previously used stationery or office paper is perfect. Writing is self-directed and can't be scheduled as a daily activity the same way that read-alouds are. But that doesn't mean it can't be encouraged.

For example, when you're writing a letter to Uncle Marc to thank him for sending a book, your child can "write" her own note, too. She can help with a shopping list or make a sign to stop a pesky brother from messing up her room. Once a child has started to "write," he or she needs little further encouragement to keep going.

At first, a child's writing won't look like writing at all—it will look more like "drawing." But soon you'll notice that some of it contains both drawings and scribbles that look like writing from afar. (The child is probably imitating adult writing or text found in books.) A little later, you'll see some letters mixed in with the scribbles. They're likely to be letters that are significant to the child, perhaps ones from his own name or ones seen in the environment. Later still, more recognizable letters appear, as do spaces between "words." Eventually, the words will have the correct initial/final consonants; the vowels are the last to arrive.

Although early writing looks like random letters on the page, most children go through predictable stages if they're allowed to write on their own and if you let them do it before they know all the letters and sounds or how to spell. This progression is quite normal, and allowing children to invent spellings at this stage has no effect on their subsequent ability to spell correctly. By the way, children at this age routinely reverse some of their letters and numbers. It's not necessarily a sign of dyslexia or learning disability and shouldn't worry you.

Some precocious children zip through these early stages and by kindergarten they are writing complete sentences. A few have barely begun to scribble. Most arrive able to write their name in some form. A typical beginning kindergartner, when asked to draw a picture and write about it, will put only a few letters down with the picture, and these letters may or may not correspond with the sounds he's trying to make.

Other than modeling writing and providing encouragement and a place and materials, what else can you do? Get magnetic letters for the refrigerator—they can serve as letters for reading and "writing." Your child can form them into names of people in the family and into other short words she knows. You can write simple messages like "I love you" and encourage her to write her own.

Some games are useful. I Spy ("I spy with my little eye something beginning with *T*"; then whoever guesses what it is starts the game over) teaches sound-symbol relationships. Preschoolers also love practicing on chalk boards or dry marker boards. But stay away from commercial workbooks at this stage. Children need to create their own drawings and stories on blank paper.

Your child might also like to dictate stories to you and watch you write them down. But don't stop the child from writing on his own. Dictating is telling stories, not writing them. Staple a number of blank sheets of paper together to make a "writing book" for him. And keep some early work in a folder (remember to date it) so you have a portfolio of his early writing development.

What do teachers expect children to be able to write when they arrive in kindergarten? Those we asked said they should be able to write their name, but that's all. They don't assume children will know letter formation or be able to spell or write words or sentences.

Math

While no one questions the merit of reading to preschoolers, the value of math before formal schooling is not as well recognized. Parents who seem to care most about math before their children go to school like the subject themselves, generally use it in their work, and convey their enthusiasm (and probably their talent in math) to their children. Consequently, their children do well in math from the very start.

Your child can learn to like math if you encourage her and give her opportunities to learn and use it. Polly Greenberg talks about the "natural math that surrounds us." Children's encounters with TV remote controls, clocks, telephones, license plates, microwave ovens, grocery stores, gas stations, and road signs all involve number recognition. Size numbers on clothes and shoes fascinate them.

There are lots of things to count: items in their collections (bottle caps, shells, pogs), stairs up on the way to bed, barns passed on a trip in the country. A refrigerator calendar is a tool for helping children recognize numbers and for counting (Johnny can mark off the passing days until his birthday, for example).

The concept of one-to-one correspondence presents itself when children set the table for dinner. If five people will be eating, the child needs to know to set out five of everything.

Sorting occurs regularly with laundry and also with collections (sorting the shells by size, color, or type). Addition and subtraction in their most basic form are introduced when Heather has four raisins on her plate, you give her two more, she eats three, and then she counts how many are left.

Finally, there's money. Your preschooler can help you count out money for the paper boy. In a restaurant, he can help count coins for the tip.

Math concepts abound in children's literature. A whole genre is devoted to counting and numbers; preschoolers will enjoy these stories and want to hear them read over and over. Among our favorites are Reeve Lindbergh's *The Midnight Farm*; Merle Peek's *The Balancing Act: A Counting Song*; Henry Pluckrose's *Know About Counting*; and Mary Rees's *Ten in a Bed*.

Some children show an unusual interest in counting, adding, making up math problems, and measuring things (or helping you measure them). They constantly ask questions about numbers and are able to do math problems assigned to older members of the family. If you have a child like this, let her develop her ability as long as she wants to learn more.

As with reading, we don't recommend lots of workbook pages. Instead, play board games that challenge math abilities, have the child help you measure in the kitchen as you prepare food, and let him create and solve his own math problems.

What expectations do kindergarten teachers have for children's math abilities? The ones we asked barely mentioned math (one said she expected children to have "number awareness"; another said she expected them to know their shapes). It's unfortunate that many teachers put so much stress on prereading skills and so little on math. That makes you think literacy is critical but numeracy isn't. But both are important. You could inadvertently stifle your child's natural inclination toward math by not giving her opportunities to investigate mathematical processes, by emphasizing literacy more, or by passing along your own negative feelings about math.

Knowledge of the World

Children acquire a remarkable amount of information about the world around them in their first four or five years. They gain some of it directly through observation and experience. Much of it comes from listening to adults who either tell what they know or pass on other people's knowledge, usually through reading. These days, children also get lots of information from the media—mostly from television, but also from the radio and sometimes through computers.

This world knowledge includes the natural and physical sciences, history, geography, culture, religion, health, and literature. Enlarging understanding in these areas is a major goal of education at all levels.

Preschoolers are naturally curious about their world—especially animals, plants, people, and places. We routinely underestimate their capacity for learning about their environment, possibly because adults so frequently equate knowledge with what's learned in school. Whatever the reason, we sometimes forget that this never-stay-still four-year-old is also a very active learner who wants to know why things happen, what things are, who did what, and what's going on. Behind those wide eyes that seem to be soaking in the world around him is a brain constantly searching out new information.

You can do things to help your child expand his knowledge of the world. Bring him information through books, audiocassettes, films or videos, even computers. For example, make sure when you read aloud that you include a healthy amount of nonfiction or that some of the fiction you choose contains good information about the world. Pick out suitable videos or watch television shows like *Reading Rainbow, Sesame Street, Bill Nye,* and *Mister Rogers' Neighborhood.* If you have a computer with a CD-ROM, there is a limited but growing set of titles suitable for very young children.

By all means, take your child to the source. Trips to museums, zoos, aquariums, or theme parks, to other parts of your state or to other states, even abroad, are marvelous opportunities for children to acquire new information. And don't ignore the possibilities close to home. As you shop, eat at a restaurant, hike on nature trails, or just walk around the neighborhood, there are many things to observe and learn about. Talk about the jobs people do, different birds in the neighborhood, the kinds of houses people live in, the fire department.

Take a lesson from Anita Sanchez and Nancy Payne of the Five Rivers Environmental Center in Delmar, New York. They encourage young children to explore nature largely through the senses rather than by simply naming things. For example, they recommend having children feel and smell different kinds of leaves and examine them up close with magnifying glasses. They suggest open-ended rather than yes-no questions: *I wonder why there's a hole in that tree. What do you think?* rather than *Look at this hole. Do you think a bird made it?"*

There are learning opportunities everywhere. You don't have

to point everything out or make every outing a science or social studies lesson. Just talk about what interests you, ask open-ended questions, and let your child's own curiosity do the rest. At home, keep a simple weather chart on the refrigerator that tracks the daily temperature, whether it was sunny, cloudy, or rainy, and how these weather conditions affected what the family did that day. Ask your child to garden with you—let him plant a few flowers or vegetables in his own little area, or simply let him dig and explore what's inside the soil. When you're planting flowers or pruning bushes, explain what you're doing. Use the technical terminology ("Pass me the dibbet, would you, Miles? I need to dig little holes for the tulip bulbs").

Finally, let your child explore and play with different kinds of objects. Containers or objects in water in the sink or bathtub teach about objects that sink or float; building blocks reveal lots of emerging scientific principles. The idea is to encourage your child to experience science and nature up close and in tangible ways. Children at this age don't really need much instruction. They need to be immersed, engaged, and encouraged.

What's the payoff for all of this? A steady assimilation of scientific, historical, and geographical knowledge and reinforcement for developing literacy abilities. The child who sees frogs in the wild gets interested in them, can make sense of books about them, and write about them if he wants to. This kind of exposure also builds vocabulary. The more words your child understands, the easier it becomes to connect them to the printed words in a book. The more he knows, the more he'll want to know. These encounters with knowledge in the world help children develop and maintain their disposition toward learning.

What will kindergarten teachers expect in this area? Curiously, none of those we asked even mentioned it. They did, however, recommend that parents take their children on trips and expose them to knowledge of the world.

Social Development

One of the biggest adjustments children have to make when they go to kindergarten is being with a fairly large number of other children for a half or full day, with only one teacher, or a teacher and an aide. But most make this transition fairly quickly. It certainly helps if a child has already been in preschool or daycare, although there are always more adults in preschool and daycare than in kindergarten.

Children who have stayed at home or been part of small play groups aren't necessarily at a disadvantage, though. It really depends on the child's personality and how well he or she adapts to new situations. Children from large families generally seem to have an easier time for obvious reasons—they've had to learn how to live with lots of siblings.

There are five aspects of social development you should consider in the year or so before kindergarten. First, it's good for children to have spent time with other children (on the playground, in play groups, daycare, preschool, YMCA, in church). That interaction teaches valuable lessons about taking turns, sharing, and just getting along with other children of the same age. The social lessons adults want children to learn don't come easily to self-centered, egocentric preschoolers. But they'll take even longer to learn if children aren't in situations where they have to interact with their peers.

Second, it really helps if preschoolers have spent some time in groups listening to adults. One good way to provide this experience is to have them attend a story hour at the local public library. Other ways include taking them to plays or other performances or to church or religious school.

Third, children need to have spent some time away from their parents. If you work, this isn't an issue because daycare and/or preschool is already an integral part of your child's life. When one or both parents are at home, however, it's a concern. Some children in these circumstances have little trouble with the separation that comes with kindergarten, while others have such anxieties they're forced to wait another year before starting. Rather than risk that, it would be much better to make sure the child spends some time away from home during his third and fourth year.

Fourth, we share the concern of Waldorf educators about the negative effects of too much television and the exposure to excessive violence that comes with it. We believe you should limit the amount of TV your preschooler watches for two reasons. First, it's essentially an antisocial activity. Time spent in front of the set is time not spent interacting with other members of the family, with adults, with other children, or with toys. Second, too much TV limits, controls, and defines a child's imagination. The more a child becomes subservient to other people's definitions of reality, the less able he is to impose and create his own. This becomes especially troublesome when violence dominates the reality portrayed on TV. There are good alternatives. *Arthur, Sesame Street, Bill Nye, Reading Rainbow* and *Mister Rogers' Neighborhood* are some outstanding examples.

On the whole, too many preschoolers are watching too much TV that has no redeeming social or educational value. And the same goes for rented videos—just how much does a child get from watching cartoon versions of fairy tales over and over again? We wish more parents had the courage to unplug the set and put it in the attic. If that seems a little drastic for you, at least severely limit viewing and hire only baby-sitters or daycare providers who don't use it as a major activity.

Fifth, while much of the concern about social development focuses on making children adapt to the norms and conventions of adults (sitting still, paying attention, sharing, and getting along with others), we think they should all be encouraged to develop unique personalities—even when this conflicts with our desire to have them obey our rules or to be just like us.

The truth is that children impose themselves on the world just as much as the world imposes itself on them. And thank goodness they do! Some are quiet and reflective; others are gregarious and loud. Some literally cannot sit still; others show little interest in movement. Some have a passion for nature; others couldn't care less about it. While we are helping children live with those around them, we shouldn't dampen developing personalities and interests in the name of conformity.

It's a different story, of course, if the child is causing physical or emotional harm to others. This tension between self-expression and conventional behavior challenges parents and early childhood educators. We don't mean that children should never be admonished for inappropriate behavior. But sometimes, adults come down too heavily on the side of behaving properly and forget to nurture the child's developing personality or simply to model appropriate behavior themselves. Two things are important here:

children actively involved in activities that genuinely interest them rarely misbehave, and they're much more likely to model good behavior if that's what they encounter in their daily lives.

What level of social development do kindergarten teachers expect? They have a lot more to say about this area than most of the others. Generally, they want children who can work and play with others their age, are able to sit and listen to an adult, and are comfortable away from their parents for part of the day.

Social immaturity is a major reason teachers recommend that a child be retained. But various kinds of kindergarten approaches have different views on socialization. Whole language and developmentally appropriate programs are far more tolerant of children with less well-developed social skills than traditional programs are, although no teacher is likely to want a homesick child in her classroom for too long. If a case of separation anxiety is particularly severe, parents are almost always asked to take the child out of the class.

Aesthetic Development

This refers to the child's interest in and use, appreciation, and understanding of literature, music, art, and drama. Howard Gardner recounts the story of Yehudi Menuhin, who at the age of three was taken to San Francisco Orchestra concerts. The child was so delighted with what he experienced that he asked for a violin for his birthday, got one, and by the age of ten was an international performer. Not all preschoolers will be on their way to becoming internationally renowned violinists, but they all will profit from attention to their aesthetic development. Sadly, this is not a major priority of most public schools. Music and art are frequent victims of budget cuts and are often treated as supplementary frills to the three R's. But they're a critical element of education and need to be nurtured early on.

You can do a lot in that regard. Good literature and poetry read aloud introduce children to great stories and expose them to rich and beautiful language. It doesn't matter that they can't fully understand everything they hear. As Robert McNeil points out, this exposure to language lays down what he calls "layers of meaning" that accumulate and form the basis for an appreciation and understanding of literature later on.

Exposing children to a variety of music—classical, modern, folk, jazz—does the same thing to their understanding and appreciation of music. If they hear only popular music, they won't know what preceded it or have any idea of the incredible range of music that is woven into the fabric of a country's culture and history. It's never too early to start children on their own musical journey, as listeners and players. Music requires only a pair of active ears and an instrument to play (not necessarily with formal lessons).

If you like classical music, smuggle your child into a concert and see what happens. Take him to a jazz festival or a folk concert. Play different kinds of music at bedtime, in the car, or while you are preparing supper. Ask your child if he likes what he hears. But don't make too big a deal of it. Music has to be heard over a long enough period to build an appreciation.

Encourage your child to make music, too. If you own a piano or electronic keyboard, let him "play" with it. Get some battery-operated toys so he can begin to play basic tunes using a color-coded system. Vocal music is available to everyone. Buy or tape some appealing music and chances are he'll soon be singing along to that and to musical videos, too.

Similarly, children need to be exposed to art in all its forms, both as spectator and participant. Young children seem to take to modern art more easily than adults do. Maybe it's because so much modern art is so striking, even childlike. A child may not remember Picasso's name, but won't easily forget cubist art or Dali's dripping clocks. A four-year-old might even wonder how a Jackson Pollock is any different from his own artistic efforts! A huge sculpture by Henry Moore outside an office building might excite a five-year-old and lead to a lifelong interest in that art form.

Make art a part of your child's life. All he needs is something to draw or paint on or sculpt with, some implements (paintbrushes, crayons, markers, his hands), and some encouragement. Library books are crammed with ideas for "craft" projects, but it's good to leave them open-ended so your child doesn't treat them simply as exercises to complete.

Preschoolers don't see other people's art very often, but we think it should be a regular part of their lives. Expose them to different kinds (paintings, sculptures), periods (ancient Egypt, Renaissance, Impressionists, modern), and cultures (European, African,

85

Native American). Children are enthralled with museums and art galleries (if the visits are brief) because they get to see the paintings and sculptures up close. Looking at the pictures in adult art books is surprisingly effective, and there are also books about art especially for children.

But don't restrict your child's notion of art to painting and sculpture. Introduce him to photography, architecture, quilts, furniture, and jewelry—whatever you both find aesthetically pleasing.

Do teachers have any expectations for children's aesthetic development as they arrive in kindergarten? We don't think so. It isn't much of a priority for most. But nurturing it will have an enormous impact on their lives.

Physical Development

In most cases, preschoolers develop according to their own physiological timetables, and if they get a normal amount of exercise and healthy food, their physical development needs very little attention.

However, certain aspects, namely gross and fine motor control, are of particular concern in traditional kindergartens. *Gross motor control* is a child's ability to control muscles that relate to activities such as running, skipping, and throwing and catching a ball. *Fine motor control* is control over muscles in the hands and wrists that govern holding a pencil or pen and writing such things as letters of the alphabet.

For a long time, conventional wisdom held that children went through developmental stages, mastering gross, then fine motor control before they could write. Since writing was a first-grade activity, fine motor control was a prerequisite to be mastered in kindergarten. Current thinking is that neither ability is a prerequisite to writing and that fine motor control develops in part as a child engages in writing, not before she starts. In other words, writing, previously believed to be impossible until a child's fine motor control was sufficiently well developed, turns out to be one of the major activities that promotes it.

Unfortunately, many teachers in traditional readiness programs (but not in whole language or developmentally appropriate

86

approaches) still believe children need gross and fine motor control exercises before they can write. We agree they are important aspects of physical development, but we don't think they're necessary for writing. We also don't think children need any special exercises (except, obviously, if there are impairments in the muscular system). Playing with small toys (such as Legos, Lincoln Logs, and miniature cars) helps develop fine motor control, as does writing.

So what does a child need before coming to school? Plenty of opportunities for outside play—walking, running, skipping, jumping, and climbing—especially with other children of their age. We agree with David Elkind, who writes in his book *Miseducation* that formal instruction in sports like tennis or skiing is unnecessary for three- and four-year-olds. They run the risk of becoming overly dependent on adults for guidance and lose some of their autonomy. If you include your preschooler in family sports, let him participate at his own level and in his own way. No harm will be done, and the child's physical development will be perfectly normal.

What do kindergarten teachers expect in terms of children's physical development? Many teachers in our survey thought the gross and fine motor skills we mentioned earlier were important.

Other Aspects

There are a few other skills we haven't yet mentioned that the majority of kindergarten teachers would like children to possess when they come to kindergarten. They'd like them to be able to:

- Use the bathroom independently (there's no delicate way to put this—children need to be able to wipe themselves, flush the toilet, and wash their hands! Boys need to be able to aim straight).
- Blow their noses and discard the tissue in the garbage can (the whole concept of blowing one's nose is harder than you might think for a five-year-old).
- Cover their mouth and nose when they sneeze or cough.
- Be able to dress themselves (be able to manage buttons, zippers, tie shoes that have laces, get shoes on the right feet).

- Know their name, phone number, and address (and know what to do if they arrive home and no one is there).
- Be able to clean up after themselves (put away toys and books and clean up after snack).

Most teachers probably won't be too upset if a few children are unable to do all of these things. The problem comes when many arrive unable to do them and the teacher is alone in the room. You can imagine how distracting it is to be interrupted while reading a story by a little voice coming from the bathroom saying, "Mrs. Camp, will you come and wipe me?"

Finally, there are three small but vital things you can do that will allow the teacher to focus on her teaching:

- Label all your child's belongings (we know *you* can recognize them, but no one else can! Your child isn't the only one whose backpack is decorated with the characters from the latest Disney movie).
- Get your child to bed early enough so that he or she gets a proper night's sleep.
- Make sure your child has a good breakfast before school.

Conclusion

TRACY

One day, you'll look through your family photographs and come across the ones you took the day your child started kindergarten. They'll bring back the pride, the fears, the uncertainties of one of life's milestones.

If you were blessed with an outgoing, well-adjusted child, probably all you felt was the hurt of separation and the bittersweet realization that one phase of your son's or daughter's childhood is ending. But for many parents, this moment is fraught with anxieties. Did I make the right choice to send Eliza? Should I have kept her back? Will her teacher be kind and accepting? Have I done everything I should have to prepare her for school? Did I choose the right program?

Kindergarten is where home and school intersect, but for too long, parents have had to figure out on their own how to make this transition work. Relying mostly on what schools chose to share with them, the gossip of neighbors and friends, and on their own school experiences, they've made the best judgments they could with limited information.

We wrote this book because you deserve to know about the different kinds of programs being offered, current issues affecting them, and how best to get information and prepare your child. We hope we've helped you navigate the murky waters between home and school.

You should now know more about the kinds of kindergartens available in public and private schools. If you were seeking information on how to prepare your child, we hope we've supported what you're already doing. If you think you've fallen short in some areas, don't panic. We'd rather have children come to kindergarten with some gaps in their experiences than having been force-fed these experiences in the months just before school starts.

We hope also you've gained confidence. Confidence about what you know, about choices you've made and those you'll be called upon to make. Confidence in expressing your views and standing your ground when someone asks you to do something—like retaining your child—that you don't think is right.

But we don't want you to be overconfident. It's vital to consider the perspectives and experiences of others. Your child's preschool teacher or day-care provider, other family members or close friends, and kindergarten teachers and other school staff all have important contributions to make.

We want to leave you with a couple of things we've learned both as parents of kindergartners, and as school consultants. One is that it's almost impossible to radically change a school's approach to kindergarten in a very short time—a couple of months before your child's first day there, for example. The other is that children are much more adaptable than we give them credit for—they often thrive in circumstances that are far from ideal. This shouldn't discourage you from raising questions and advocating change in your school district, but you do need to be realistic about the time it will take to bring these changes about. In the meantime, use this book—and the other sources we recommend—to make informed decisions about which kind of kindergarten you want for your child and about how best to prepare your child for this important year. And if you can help make your school's kindergarten an even better experience for children not yet enrolled, so much the better!

Here's wishing you and your child a great kindergarten year. We hope you both get off to a good start!

Endnotes

The notes below direct you to sources you can consult if you'd like to explore kindergarten issues in greater depth. To help you find the information you want more easily, we've arranged the materials under sections that correspond with the sections in Chapters 1 and 2. Full bibliographic information for all the sources mentioned is included in the References.

Learning More About Different Kinds of Kindergarten

We are sometimes surprised that colleagues in schools and universities know little about alternatives to traditional kindergartens, so you shouldn't be too upset if you haven't heard of them either. Here are some useful sources on different kinds of kindergarten, so you can explore them on your own.

Whole Language

If you've only heard about whole language in the newspapers or on talk radio, you may have the impression that it's a loosey-goosey approach in which children do whatever they want, while teachers just observe and never teach them skills. This is a gross misrepresentation of an approach whose roots stretch back to Rousseau and Dewey. The only way we know to correct these distortions is to read about whole language from the people who started this movement and who advocate it. We recommend Kenneth Goodman's *What's Whole in Whole Language?* for a brief but clear introduction to whole language. *Whole Language: What's the Difference?* by Edelsky, Altwerger, and Flores is good too. The best books we know that describe whole language kindergarten classrooms are Bobbi Fisher's *Joyful Learning: A Whole Language Kindergarten* and Raines and Canady's *The Whole Language Kindergarten*. For an interesting account of a kindergarten teacher's transition to a whole language kindergarten, see Connie White's book *Jevon Doesn't Sit at the Back Anymore*.

Developmentally Appropriate

Two books from the National Association for the Education of Young Children (NAEYC) will help you understand their developmentally appropriate approach. Sue Bredekamp's *Developmentally Appropriate Practice in Early Childhood Programs Serving Children from Birth Through Age 8* is a comprehensive statement of NAEYC's approach to early childhood education. Peck, McCaig, and Sapp's *Kindergarten Policies: What Is Best for Children?* reviews many of the issues surrounding traditional and developmentally appropriate kindergartens. So does Anne McGill-Franzen in her article "Early Literacy: What Does Developmentally Appropriate Mean?" David Elkind's article "Developmentally Appropriate Practice: Philosophical and Practical Implications" also deals with these issues. You may wish to browse through current and back issues of *Young Children*, the professional journal of the NAEYC, and review its publications (write them at 1834 Connecticut Ave. NW, Washington, DC 20009-5786 for their most recent catalog—they have many publications for parents as well as early childhood educators). A good discussion of how schools can change from traditional to developmentally appropriate kindergartens is Goffin and Stegelin's *Changing Kindergartens*.

To learn more about the Reggio Emilia approach to early childhood education, we'd recommend you read Carolyn Edwards et. al.'s *The Hundred Languages of Children: The Reggio Emilia Approach to Early Childhood Education* and Lella Gandini's "Fundamentals of the Reggio Emilia Approach to Early Childhood Education."

Our own approach to a developmentally appropriate kindergarten is described in two recent books. *Teaching Kindergarten: A*

Developmentally Appropriate Approach describes our philosophy and practice. *Teaching Kindergarten: A Theme-Centered Curriculum* lays out our curriculum.

Montessori
We suggest you write to the American Montessori Society (150 Fifth Avenue, New York, NY 10011) for a list of their publications. The AMS supports a modern, reformed Montessori approach. If you're interested in the original, "purist" Montessori philosophy, then contact the Association Montessori Internationale (7211 Regency Square Blvd., Suite 215, Houston, TX 77036). As far as books are concerned, we learned a great deal from the late Nancy Rambusch's *Learning How to Learn: An American Approach to Montessori* and from Elizabeth Hainstock's *Essential Montessori*. If you're willing to work a little harder, we think Maria Montessori's own writings are fascinating, although they're written in a difficult and rather flowery style. Start with *Dr. Montessori's Own Handbook*, and if that fascinates you, tackle *The Montessori Method*, her major statement of her philosophy. An interesting recent book is Lesley Britton's *Montessori Play and Learn: A Parent's Guide to Purposeful Play from Two to Six*. Finally, there's a magazine, *Tomorrow's Child*, which is published six times a year by the Montessori Foundation (17808 October Court, Rockville, MD 20855).

Waldorf
To learn more about Waldorf schools, write the Association of Waldorf Schools of North America (3911 Bannister Road, Fair Oaks, CA 95628) or the Waldorf Kindergarten Association (7303 Dartmouth Avenue, College Park, MD 20740). The Anthroposophic Press (Bell's Pond, Star Route, Hudson, NY 12534) will send you a list of Waldorf-related books and pamphlets. We found Rahima Baldwin's *You Are Your Child's First Teacher* very helpful in explaining the Waldorf philosophy. Baldwin gives many suggestions for parents who want to nurture their preschoolers' development according to Waldorf principles. You might also want to read some of Rudolph Steiner's own writings—his *Introduction to Waldorf Education,* for example. A recent article that gives a clear picture of the Waldorf approach is *Waldorf Education: Schooling the*

Head, Hands and Heart, which is available directly from the author (Ronald Kotzsch, P.O. Box 3382, Amherst, MA 01004).

Learning More About Kindergarten Issues

In Chapter 2, we deliberately made few references to specific research studies or books so that you wouldn't be constantly interrupted. Here, we'll give details of those studies, as well as further reading you might want to do.

Entry Age

This topic is discussed in some detail in Chapter 1 of *Kindergarten Policies: What Is Best for Children?* (Peck, McCaig, and Sapp). David Elkind makes a very strong case for not hurrying the preschool child along too fast in his book *The Hurried Child*; more recently, in *Miseducation,* he warns parents against holding a child out of school to ensure later academic or sports success. Both books are easy to read and make compelling arguments.

Readiness

To learn more about the work of Arnold Gesell, we recommend that you read *The Mental Growth of the Preschool Child,* which he wrote in 1925, and also Ilg and Ames's *School Readiness.* William S. Gray's 1927 article called "Training and Experiences that Prepare for Reading" explains the origins of the traditional readiness kindergarten. Debbie May and Debbie Kundert (1992) have found that as many as 50 percent of all schools in New York State still recommend giving children an extra year (the "gift of time") when school personnel they think aren't ready to begin school. For a reappraisal of the concept of readiness, you'll find Graue's (1993) book *Ready for What?* particularly interesting, as is Sharon Kagan's recent article "Readiness Past, Present, and Future." A recent article by Debbie May and her colleagues (1994) entitled "School Readiness: An Obstacle to Intervention and Inclusion" provides an interesting commentary on this issue from a special education perspective.

As we said in Chapter 2, the notion of readiness has given way to the notion of emergent literacy. The term *emergent literacy* comes originally from the New Zealand educator Marie Clay. It is well described in Leslie Morrow's book *Literacy Development in the Early Years* and in Teale and Sulzby's *Emergent Literacy: Writing and Reading*. Another very readable book on emergent literacy is Judith Schickedanz's *More Than the ABCs: The Early Stages of Reading and Writing*.

Retention
The best resource we know—and it's the one that everyone quotes—is Shepard and Smith's *Flunking Grades: Research and Policies on Retention*. We'd also recommend the highly readable "Flunking: Throwing Good Money After Bad," by Richard Allington and Anne McGill-Franzen. Evidence that assigning children to prefirst or transitional programs doesn't work can be found in May and Kundert's "Prefirst Placements: How Common and How Informed?" There's also interesting evidence about some negative effects of holding children out to avoid retention in May, Kundert, and Brent's "Does Delayed School Entry Reduce Later Grade Retentions and Use of Special Education Services?"

Meeting the Needs of Advanced Learners
The story about Yehudi Menuhin came from Howard Gardner's book *Multiple Intelligences*. Another book of Gardner's, *The Unschooled Mind*, is also a great resource for parents to reflect on what it means to be intelligent. To learn more about giftedness in young children, we suggest you contact the Center for Talented Youth (The Johns Hopkins University, 3400 N. Charles St., Baltimore, MD 21218) and the National Research Center on Gifted and Talented (University of Connecticut, 362 Fairfield Road U-7, Storrs, CT 06269) and request a list of their publications. The Center for Talented Youth publishes the *Sourcebook for Parents of Intellectually Gifted Preschool and Elementary School Children*. We also recommend you write the National Association for Gifted Children (1155 15th NW, Suite 1002, Washington, DC 20005) and the Council for Exceptional Children (1920 Association Drive, Reston, VA 22091). Both have publications for parents. A highly readable book by Sally Walker, *The Survival Guide for Parents of Gifted Kids*, is full of useful information. Klein and Tannenbaum's book *To Be Young and Gifted* goes into this topic more deeply.

Meeting the Needs of At-risk Children

Denny Taylor's *Learning Denied* comes to mind immediately when we think of meeting the needs of at-risk children. We'd also recommend Allington and Walmsley's *No Quick Fix: Rethinking Literacy Programs in America's Elementary Schools.*

Half-day versus Full-day Kindergarten

There's an excellent discussion of this topic in Peck, McCaig, and Sapp's *Kindergarten Policies: What Is Best for Children?* (pages 64–67). They also provide a bibliography for further reading.

Class Size

For NAEYC's recommendations on class size, see Bredekamp's *Developmentally Appropriate Practice in Early Childhood Programs Serving Children From Birth Through Age 8* (page 57). The new study on class size we referred to is "The Tennessee Study of Class Size in the Early School Grades," by Frederick Mosteller. For another perspective on this issue, see Slavin's recent "School and Classroom Organization in Beginning Reading."

Multiage

The best book we know on multiage is Anne Bingham's *Exploring the Multiage Classroom.* Although it's written primarily for teachers, it gives parents an excellent overview of multiage classrooms. Montessori schools have always advocated multiage classrooms, and so you'll find useful information on multiage in the books about Montessori.

Teacher Experience and Qualifications

The topic of kindergarten teacher experience and qualifications is not often discussed in the professional literature, as far as we can tell. The NAEYC guidelines on developmentally appropriate practice (Bredekamp 1987) state that teachers who work with five-through eight-year-olds should have a degree in early childhood education or in elementary education with a specialty in early childhood, as well as supervised field experience with this age group. They should also take periodic professional development courses, seminars, and workshops.

Screening Before Kindergarten, Testing During Kindergarten

This topic is extensively covered in Peck, McCaig, and Sapp's *Kindergarten Policies: What Is Best for Children?* (pages 15–30). We'd also recommend Samuel Meisels's *Developmental Screening in Early Childhood: A Guide* and his "Uses and Abuses of Developmental Screening and School Readiness Tests."

Parental Involvement

Polly Greenberg's article "Parents as Partners in Young Children's Development and Education" is an excellent place to begin—she puts parental involvement into perspective and explains why schools have until recently been so reluctant to involve parents in their child's education. This topic is also well covered in Peck, McCaig, and Sapp's *Kindergarten Policies: What Is Best for Children?*

References

Allington, R. L. and P. Cunningham. 1996. *Schools That Work: Where All Children Read and Write*. New York: HarperCollins.

Allington, R. L. and A. McGill-Franzen. 1995. "Flunking: Throwing Good Money After Bad." In *No Quick Fix: Redesigning Literacy Programs in America's Elementary Schools*, ed. R. L. Allington and Sean A. Walmsley. 45–60. New York: Teachers College Press.

Allington, R. L. and S. A. Walmsley, eds. 1995. *No Quick Fix: Redesigning Literacy Programs in America's Elementary Schools*. New York: Teachers College Press/International Reading Association.

American Guidance Service. 1995. *Dial-R: Developmental Indicators for the Assessment of Learning (Revised)*. Circle Pines, MN: American Guidance Service.

Baldwin, R. 1989. *You Are Your Child's First Teacher*. Berkeley, CA: Celestial Arts.

Bingham, A. A. 1995. *Exploring the Multiage Classroom*. York, ME: Stenhouse Publishers.

Bram, E. 1977. *I Don't Want to Go to School*. New York: Greenwillow.

Bredekamp, S. 1987. *Developmentally Appropriate Practice in Early Childhood Programs Serving Children from Birth Through Age 8*. Washington, DC: National Association for the Education of Young Children.

Brigance, A. 1982. *Brigance K and 1 Screen for Kindergarten and First Grade*. North Billerica, MA: Curriculum Associates.

Britton, L. 1992. *Montessori Play and Learn: A Parent's Guide to Purposeful Play From Two to Six*. New York: Crown.

Butler, D. and M. M. Clay. 1987. *Reading Begins at Home*. 2nd Edition. Portsmouth, NH: Heinemann.

Caudill, R. 1964. *A Pocketful of Cricket*. New York: Rinehart.

Cohen, M. 1967. *Will I Have a Friend?* New York: Macmillan.

Doake, D. B. 1988. *Reading Begins at Birth*. New York: Scholastic.

Edelsky, C., B. Altwerger, and B. Flores. 1990. *Whole Language: What's the Difference?* Portsmouth, NH: Heinemann.

Edwards, C., L. Gandini, and G. Forman, eds. 1993. *The Hundred Languages of Children: The Reggio Emilia Approach to Early Childhood Education*. Norwood, NJ: Ablex.

Elkind, D. 1981. *The Hurried Child: Growing up Too Fast, Too Soon*. Reading, MA: Addison-Wesley.

Elkind, D. 1987. *Miseducation: Preschoolers at Risk*. New York: Knopf.

Elkind, D. 1989. "Developmentally Appropriate Practice: Philosophical and Practical Implications." *Phi Delta Kappan* 71 (2): 113–117.

Fisher, B. 1991. *Joyful Learning: A Whole Language Kindergarten*. Portsmouth, NH: Heinemann.

Gandini, L. 1993. Fundamentals of the Reggio Emilia Approach to Early Childhood Education. *Young Children* 49(1): 4–8.

Gardner, H. 1991. *The Unschooled Mind: How Children Think and How Schools Should Teach*. New York: Basic Books.

Gardner, H. 1993. *Multiple Intelligences: The Theory in Practice*. New York: Basic Books.

Gesell, A. L. 1925. *The Mental Growth of the Pre-school Child*. NY: Macmillan.

Goffin, S. G. and D. A. Stegelin, eds. 1992. *Changing Kindergartens*. Washington, DC: National Association for the Education of Young Children.

Goodman, K. S. 1986. *What's Whole in Whole Language?* Portsmouth, NH: Heinemann.

Graue, M. E. 1993. *Ready for What? Constructing Meanings of Readiness for Kindergarten.* Albany, NY: SUNY Press.

Gray, W. S. 1927. "Training and Experiences That Prepare for Reading." *Childhood Education* 3:213.

Greenberg, P. 1989. "Parents as Partners in Young Children's Development and Education: A New American Fad? Why Does it Matter?" *Young Children* 44(4): 61–74.

Greenberg, P. 1993. "How and Why to Teach all Aspects of Pre-school and Kindergarten Math Naturally, Democratically, and Effectively." *Young Children* 48(4): 75–84.

Hainstock, E. 1986. *Essential Montessori.* New York: New American Library.

Hamilton-Merritt, J. 1982. *My First Days of School.* New York: Simon and Schuster.

Houghton Mifflin. 1991. *Houghton Mifflin Literature Experience.* Boston, MA: Houghton Mifflin.

Howe, J. 1994. *When You Go to Kindergarten.* New York: Morrow Junior Books.

Ilg, F. L. and L. B. Ames. 1972. *School Readiness.* New York: Harper & Row.

Kagan, S. L. 1992. "Readiness Past, Present, and Future: Shaping the Agenda." *Young Children* 48(1): 48–53.

Klein, P. S. and A. Tannenbaum, eds. 1992. *To Be Young and Gifted.* Norwood, NJ: Ablex.

Kotzsch, R. E. 1989. "Waldorf Education: Schooling the Head, Hands and Heart." *East West* 19(5): 68–72, 98–101.

Larrick, N. 1982. *A Parents' Guide to Children's Reading.* New York: Bantam.

Lindbergh, R. 1995. *The Midnight Farm.* New York: Puffin Pied Piper.

Lipson, E. 1991. *New York Times Parents' Guide to the Best Books for Children.* New York: Times Books.

May, D. C. and D. K. Kundert. 1992. "Prefirst Placements: How Common and How Informed?" *Psychology in the Schools* 30: 161–167.

May, D. C., D. K. Kundert, and D. Brent. 1995. "Does Delayed School Entry Reduce Later Grade Retentions and Use of Special Education Services?" *Remedial and Special Education* 16 (5): 288–294.

May, D. C., D. K. Kundert, O. Nikoloff, E. Welch, M. Garrett, and D. Brent. 1994. "School Readiness: An Obstacle to Intervention and Inclusion." *Journal of Early Intervention* 18 (3): 290–301.

McGill-Franzen, A. 1992. "Early Literacy: What Does Developmentally Appropriate' Mean?" *The Reading Teacher* 46(1): 56–58.

McNeil, R. 1989. *Wordstruck: A Memoir*. New York: Viking.

Meisels, S. J. 1985. *Developmental Screening in Early Childhood: A Guide*. Revised ed. Washington, DC: National Association for the Education of Young Children.

Meisels, S. J. 1987. "Uses and Abuses of Developmental Screening and School Readiness Tests." *Young Children* 42(2): 4–6, 68–73.

Montessori, M. 1964. *The Montessori Method*. New York: Schocken.

Montessori, M. 1965. *Dr. Montessori's Own Handbook*. New York: Schocken.

Morrow, L. M. 1989. *Literacy Development in the Early Years*. Englewood Cliffs, NJ: Prentice-Hall.

Mosteller, F. 1995. The Tennessee Study of Class Size in the Early School Grades. *Critical Issues for Children and Youths* 5(2): 113–127.

New Dimensions in Education Inc. 1969. *Alphatime*. New York: New Dimensions in Education Inc.

Peck, J. T., G. McCaig, and M. E. Sapp. 1988. *Kindergarten Policies: What Is Best For Children?* Washington, DC: National Association for the Education of Young Children.

Peek, M. 1987. *The Balancing Act: A Counting Song*. New York: Clarion.

Pluckrose, H. 1988. *Know About Counting*. New York: Franklin Watts.

Raines, S. C. and R. J. Canady. 1990. *The Whole Language Kindergarten*. New York: Teachers College Press.

Rambusch, N. M. 1962. *Learning How to Learn: An American Approach to Montessori.* Baltimore, MD: Helicon Press.

Rees, M. 1988. *Ten in a Bed.* Boston, MA: Little, Brown.

Schickendanz, J. A. 1986. *More Than the ABCs: The Early Stages of Reading and Writing.* Washington, DC: National Association for the Education of Young Children.

Senisi, E. B. 1994. *Kindergarten Kids.* New York: Cartwheel Books.

Shepard, L. A. and M. L. Smith, eds. 1989. *Flunking Grades: Research and Policies on Retention.* Philadelphia: Falmer.

Slavin, R. E. 1994. "School and Classroom Organization in Beginning Reading: Class Size, Aides, and Instructional Grouping." In *Preventing Early School Failure: Research, Policy, and Practice*, ed. R. E. Slavin, N. L. Karweit, and B. A. Wasik. 122–142. Boston: Allyn Bacon.

Smith, F. 1987. *Joining the Literacy Club.* Portsmouth, NH: Heinemann.

Steiner, R. 1985. *An Introduction to Waldorf Education.* Spring Valley, NY: Anthroposophic Press.

Taylor, D. 1991. *Learning Denied.* Portsmouth, NH: Heinemann.

Teale, W. H. and E. Sulzby, eds. 1986. *Emergent Literacy: Writing and Reading.* Norwood, NJ: Ablex.

Tough, J. 1974. *Talking, Thinking, Growing: Language With the Young Child.* New York: Schocken.

Trelease, J. 1995. *Read-aloud Handbook.* 4th ed. New York: Viking-Penguin.

Walker, S. Y. 1991. *The Survival Guide for Parents of Gifted Kids.* Minneapolis, MN: Free Spirit Publishing.

Walmsley, B. D., A. M. Camp, and S. A. Walmsley. 1992a. *Teaching Kindergarten: A Developmentally Appropriate Approach.* Portsmouth, NH: Heinemann.

Walmsley, B. D., A. M. Camp, and S. A. Walmsley. 1992b. *Teaching Kindergarten: A Theme-Centered Curriculum.* Portsmouth, NH: Heinemann.

Waterland, L. 1995. *The Bridge to School: Entering a New World.* York, ME: Stenhouse Publishers.

Wells, R. 1983. *Timothy Goes to School*. New York: Puffin Pied Piper.

White, C. 1990. *Jevon Doesn't Sit at the Back Anymore*. New York: Scholastic.